Advance Praise for *Last Things*

"Loving, moving, and articulate, *Last Things* is packed with emotional truth. It's a clear-eyed testimony to the way death arrives, sometimes inch by inch, inspiring the courage and strength and generosity that are the best things we bring to this life."

—Jennifer Hayden, Eisner-nominated author of *Underwire* and *The Story of My Tits*

"Before reading Marissa Moss' *Last Things* I was unaware of how profoundly moved I could be by a graphic novel. With her gentle touch and brave honest voice, we experience how completely one's life and expectations can be changed with a single devastating diagnosis. I absolutel y loved *Last Things*!"

—Luisa Smith, Book Passage

"A gripping portrayal of how devastating ALS can be, but also a powerful example of resilience and hope."

—Dr. Catherine Lomen-Hoerth, neurologist, ALS clinic, UCSF

"If anyone still thinks the graphic format can't be used to tell deep, grown-up, powerful stories, *Last Things* ought to change their mind. It's about all the big questions: How we live, how we raise our children, how we survive seemingly unbearable loss. Moss's authenticity, raw honesty and vulnerability will help anyone who's struggling with loss and 'lasts'—ultimately, that's all of us."

—Marjorie Ingall, author of *Mamaleh Knows Best*

"For every person affected by ALS, there is a story to tell. From her front-line perspective, Marissa Moss bravely shares her family's challenges during her husband's journey with ALS in a very personal way. We are grateful for her efforts to raise awareness and support for people living with ALS and their families."

—The ALS Association Golden West Chapter

"With expressive drawings and an earnest reflective voice, Marissa Moss creates real intimacy with her readers, bringing them into this personal story of disease, heartbreak, and love. *Last Things* testifies to the redemptive power of memory, history, and writing."

—Amy Kurzweil, author of *The Flying Couch*

"Powerful and beautiful—this book is a great addition to the graphic memoir canon."

—Ian Lendler, author of *The Stratford Zoo Midnight Revue Presents MacBeth*

"I was swept into the story, swept along."—Joan Lester, author of *Mama's Child*

"This is a very brave and beautifully drawn account. Anyone coping with the loss of a spouse is going to benefit—and any reader can relate to the family dynamics, the stress of caregiving, and the crisis of a terminal disease."

—Eleanor Vincent, author of *Swimming with Maya: A Mother's Story*

Last Things

a graphic memoir of loss and love

Marissa Moss

Conari Press

Artwork by Marissa Moss
Cover and interior design by Simon Stahl
Original font created by Simon Stahl

Illustration page 25: *Lou Gehrig: The Luckiest Man* by David A. Adler.
Copyright © 1997 by Terry Widener. Cover reproduction used by permission from Houghton Mifflin Harcourt Publishing Company. All rights reserved.

Conari Press
Distributed by Red Wheel/Weiser, LLC
www.redwheelweiser.com

Sign up for our newsletter and special offers by going to
www.redwheelweiser.com/newsletter/

ISBN: 978-1-57324-698-9

Library of Congress Control Number: 2016959030

Printed in the United States of America

EBM

10 9 8 7 6 5 4 3 2 1

To Harvey, always.

Preface

This is a book about loss, but also about profound love. Anyone who has faced catastrophic illness will recognize in these pages that this is also a book about living, about the strong bonds of family and how they can sustain us through impossible situations. By sharing this story, I hope readers will experience our pain, be witnesses to it, and come out stronger for it.

When my husband was first diagnosed with ALS, we didn't have time to come to terms with the diagnosis, but were immediately plunged into a steep descent, ricocheting from crisis to crisis. I didn't have the chance then to think about what it all meant. All I could do was react to the emergencies facing us. I started writing this memoir to sort it all out with words and pictures, since that's how I think, how I've approached my children's books. I needed to shape the whirlwind we had lived through so I could understand it better, so I could see that I had done what I could, and move beyond the inevitable guilt. In many ways, this is a portrait of marriage, how it can sustain and abandon us, how families heal themselves, and how to cling to a sense of self in the face of medical horrors and mind-numbing bureaucracy.

So there's heartbreak in these pages, but also universal truth. We all have the capacity to face adversity, to come through it, and to heal. We all think we know how to live good lives. What's trickier is how to handle death, how to be with the dying and hold their pain and fear in our hearts. And then let them go.

— Marissa Moss

Things we're grateful for:

The sun on St. Peter's dome.

Walking home over Bernini's Bridge of Angels.

A glass of good wine.

Boys sleeping peacefully.

A full moon.

A marriage that holds your life.

So what happens when an immense boulder drops from the sky, smashing the two of you apart? Or when a thick, oily shadow covers everything good with its tainted smell? Something bad is coming, you can feel it in your bones.

And suddenly you feel very much alone. What is there to be grateful for then?

AUGUST

It's the end of our sabbatical year in Rome when things start to go wrong.

Harvey is a medieval art historian who was a curator at the Met Museum in New York and now teaches full time. Besides publishing articles and book chapters, he's been working on a book about King Louis IX's personal prayer book for as long as we've been married, sixteen years.

Louis IX, also known as Saint Louis, was the crusader king who brought Christ's crown of thorns to Paris from the Holy Land in the 13th century.

We should have spent the year in Paris, but we'd already lived there and went back often.

We wanted the chance to live someplace new. Rome housed a great French archive and library. Plus, it offered a warmer home for our three sons.

The year in Rome had been useful for Harvey's research and it had given me the material I needed for my next children's book.

And we'd all loved exploring the city.

But why is Harvey so tired all the time now?

Back home in Berkeley, Harvey sees more doctors. Now I know something is wrong.
Who would see all these "ists" if they could help it?
Some doctors you don't want to see — ever!

Proctologist

Pulmonologist

Speech Pathologist

Internist

Cardiologist

And there are adjustments to life in California again.

Elias needs supplies for his pushcart project.

Asa needs help.

I didn't learn American money in kindergarten. In Rome they don't have nickels or pennies or quarters.

Simon doesn't need anything, but the preparations for his bar mitzvah are a lot of work. And I don't mean studies.

Harvey, the son of Eastern European immigrants, is so proud of his oldest child's bar mitzvah, he's consumed with all the details, determined that everything be perfect.

Chaya, died in Chodorow, before the Nazi invasion.

Pepi, shot in Bobryka by Nazis.

Moses, died in Auschwitz.

Nathan, died in Auschwitz.

Rosa, died in Auschwitz.

Chana, survived in Palestine.

Solomon, survived in Denver, Colorado.

Harvey's father, Isadore, survived in Dallas, Texas.

Harvey's grandfather, Samuel, died in Auschwitz.

What do you think of pesto puff pastry for the appetizer? And what color for the tablecloths and napkins?

I thought the point of living in Berkeley was that you don't have to care about these kinds of things.

But my family is from Dallas. There's a different standard there.

Then you decide! I have absolutely no idea what's Dallas-worthy.

Although Cleo, my older sister, isn't from Dallas. . .

What's the theme of the bar mitzvah? Star Wars? The lottery?

Judaism.

You do it all, Harvey — please! I hate this stuff!

FLOWERS
RENTAL
MENU

Then I feel guilty that I've dumped all the work on him. Maybe that's what's making his stutter worse?

Your brother, Sid, could read your talk to Simon at the bar mitzvah.

N . . n . . . n . . no! I'm his father. It's m . . . m . . . m . . m . . MY job!

When we got married, Harvey had organized everything then, too. He was a university professor. I waited tables.

He's marrying a waitress?

She's younger, isn't she?

But to Harvey, I was a children's book writer and illustrator who hadn't been published . . . yet.

What do you think?

It's really good.

He had faith in me when no one else did.

FORGET IT!

Are you kidding?

NO WAY!

FUTURE BATHROOM WALLPAPER

NOPE!

It took five years to get that first book published, but he never lost hope. He believed in me more than I did myself.

Maybe I should give up and get a real job. I can't wait tables forever.

You're a writer, an artist. Keep at it. It'll happen.

It's my turn to have faith in him, to know that we can deal with whatever's causing the stutter. He's always taken care of so much.

When Elias had whooping cough.

The steam from the shower will help you, cutie.

Arranging the move, the apartment, the school, everything for the year in Rome.

ART SUPPLIES

TOYS

BOOKS   BOOKS

And of course, Simon's bar mitzvah.

Here's the menu.

Perfect.

You haven't looked!

It's still perfect.

By the time of the bar mitzvah, Harvey is weak and thin. But he pulls off his part — perfectly.

I'm so proud of you!

Thanks, Dad!

The connection between Simon and Harvey is so intense I'm almost jealous.

That night at the party, surrounded by friends and family, I say the familiar prayer, the Shehecheyanu, thanking God for allowing us to reach this moment.
And I mean it.

Yay, Asa!

Yay for you, Simon!

It's the last time Harvey will speak clearly.
The last time we'll celebrate together as a family.
I can feel something dark lurking under the joy, much as I try to push it away.

The next day . . .

Gasp! I can't breathe!

Gasp! Is this what one of your asthma attacks feels like?

Gasp!

At the E.R., the doctor is a neurologist. And like all the others, he has no idea what's wrong.

All I can say is that it's a neurological problem.

But what IS it?

When the boys visit, the hospital room becomes fun, not scary, at least not as long as they're there.

I brought you The New York Times, Dad.

This Jell-O is yummy!

Your bed moves — watch!

Pretty cool, huh?

The Berkeley hospital doesn't have a neurology department, but insurance won't pay for out-of-network care. As if we have a choice! A friend, a doctor in San Francisco with its top neurology department, puts in a word to get us an appointment there with Dr. Reichmann. He's a noted neurologist who sees very few new patients. We're told how lucky Harvey is to get accepted, even if we have to pay out of pocket.

Except Dr. Reichmann is clearly irritated to see us.

TICK TICK TICK TICK

This isn't a neurological problem at all.

Harvey is too tired to argue, so I do.

But his speech is slurred and he can't breathe.

He has a stutter, not a slur.

Maybe it's not slurred now, but it is sometimes.

BRRRGGG!

He lets us know our time is up.

As we drive home, we're more relieved than annoyed. Definitely not neurological is a good thing.

You never ask me to drive. Are you okay?

Just tired.

So when Dr. Reichmann calls the next day, I'm surprised.

You said it's not neurological.

I didn't have the test results from Berkeley then. I do now. Your husband needs an EMG, a test of how his muscles respond to electrical stimulus.

Why? What's wrong?

It could be something treatable, like myasthenia gravis, an auto-immune disorder.

Or?

Or it could be ALS, amyotrophic lateral sclerosis.

He speaks without changing his tone or manner.

ALS?! Lou Gehrig's disease?

Yes. Press 1 to schedule the test, press 2 to contact insurance, press 3 to start all over.

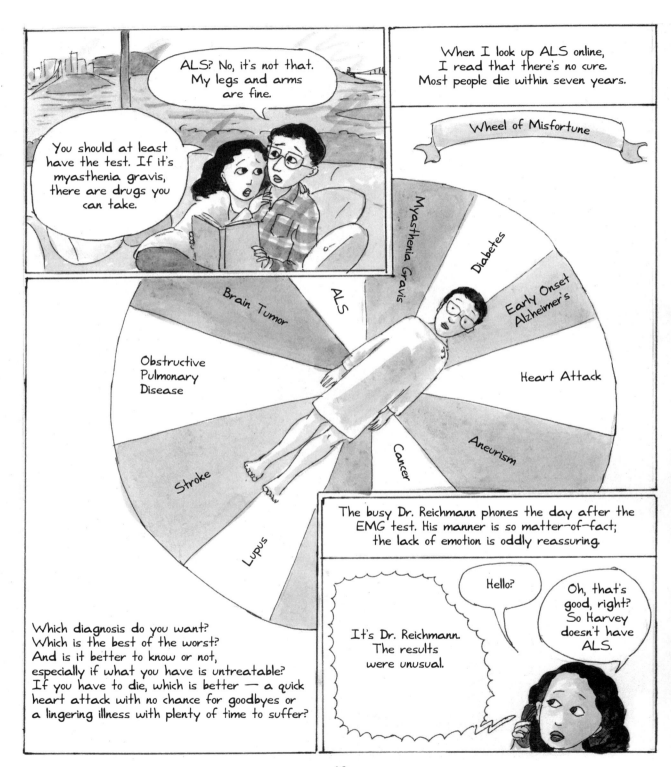

ALS? No, it's not that. My legs and arms are fine.

You should at least have the test. If it's myasthenia gravis, there are drugs you can take.

When I look up ALS online, I read that there's no cure. Most people die within seven years.

Wheel of Misfortune

Myasthenia Gravis

Diabetes

Early Onset Alzheimer's

Heart Attack

Aneurism

Cancer

Lupus

Stroke

Obstructive Pulmonary Disease

Brain Tumor

ALS

Which diagnosis do you want?
Which is the best of the worst?
And is it better to know or not,
especially if what you have is untreatable?
If you have to die, which is better — a quick heart attack with no chance for goodbyes or a lingering illness with plenty of time to suffer?

The busy Dr. Reichmann phones the day after the EMG test. His manner is so matter-of-fact; the lack of emotion is oddly reassuring.

It's Dr. Reichmann. The results were unusual.

Hello?

Oh, that's good, right? So Harvey doesn't have ALS.

10

It's shock, I tell myself. Later we'll cry together, hold each other.

Sorry isn't good enough!

But we don't. I'm sealed off in the Land of the Not-Dying.

Isn't terminal illness supposed to build stronger bonds, renewed appreciation? But this isn't like *Love Story* or *Ghost* or even *Tuesdays with Morrie.*

It's a chilly isolation, one that's strangely familiar.

I remember my mother lightly touching the top of my head. I was seven. It's the only gesture of affection from her I can recall.

Being with Harvey, held by his immense love and tender care, had rescued me from that coldness.

Now here it is **again.** I don't even question it. It's so familiar on a deep gut level. It's what I know best — you have to rely on yourself because no one else will take care of you.

It was true when I was a child. It's true **again** now.

I'm not **mad** at Harvey.
How can I be when he's the one who's **dying?**

I'm so sorry.

Go away.

But I miss him. He's the one I'd turn to for help with all this. Only I can't. I have to face it all alone.

Shut the door behind you.

Is he afraid? He must be. I can't imagine life without him.
I feel like my bones will melt under my skin.

Mom?

Is something wrong?

I used to wonder how people could live in a war zone, how they could still cook meals, do laundry.

Now I know that's when the ordinary rhythms of daily life matter most.

That's all that holds me up now, the illusion of normalcy.

At least I have groceries!

When nothing is normal now.

When are we going to tell the boys? They sense something is wrong.

Not yet.

When?

When I'm ready.

He's not ready? What happened to us, to making decisions together?

How can I complain? He's the one who's dying. How can so much change and the world still looks the same?

I can't keep this secret — it's too big.
You can tell your family and I'll tell mine. But *not* the boys. And not the university.
Good night.
Good night.
I thought I'd feel better if I told people. But I don't. It's worse, in fact. Saying the words makes them real.
Harvey has ALS, Lou Gehrig's disease.
We'll help, don't worry.
My younger sister Shelah works with autistic kids and has lots of practical suggestions. She knows how to handle insurance hassles and recommends getting a case manager to cut through red tape.
If you want us to take the boys, we will.
Steven, my other brother, is busy with his own baby, but always happy to spend time with his nephews.
?!
Brion, my youngest brother, is overwhelmed with a newborn, doesn't know what to say.
We've all gotta die sometime.
My older sister Cleo is her usual tactless self.
My parents are also in shock.

Everyone asks the same question — how are the boys taking it?

Or do they?
They must
know *something*.

How can I look at our sons with an honest, open heart when I'm hiding that kind of secret?

I can't.

It's a dreary winter day when we go to our first appointment at the ALS clinic.
Lucky for us there's one in San Francisco, at UCSF. People come from all over the state.
For us, it's just across the Bay. How convenient.

Abandon All Hope, Ye Who Enter Here

New Patients

ALS Clinic

We wait alone in the new patient's lobby.
Are we kept from the others so we won't see our future?

Harvey is charming and warm to all the doctors, his old familiar self.

Cathy, the neurologist — I wonder why a young woman would choose a specialty where all her patients will die? Why isn't she jaded or cynical?

Erin, the respiratory therapist, is also young. She's both gentle and no— nonsense.

Sharon, the speech pathologist. Another young woman. She shows Harvey exercises that will help him speak and eat.

An ALS Primer

(from bad to worse)

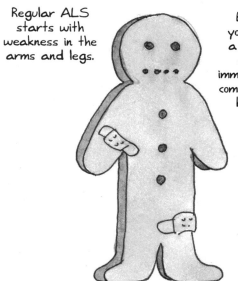

Regular ALS starts with weakness in the arms and legs.

Eventually you end up in a wheelchair, completely immobile. You can communicate only by blinking.

The diaphragm muscles are the last to go. When you can't breathe, you die, usually five to seven years after the diagnosis. For some reason, bladder and bowel muscles (and erections) aren't affected. This really matters to Harvey. He draws the line at the indignity of adult diapers.

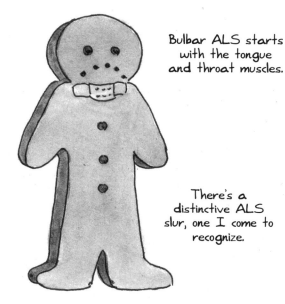

Bulbar ALS starts with the tongue and throat muscles.

There's a distinctive ALS slur, one I come to recognize.

Breathing muscles may weaken before the arms and legs, though not always. Death is generally two years after the diagnosis.

Harvey not only has Bulbar ALS, his diaphragm is already weak. Cathy warns us that it takes a year for the enormity of the diagnosis to sink in before the patient can deal with their new reality. That's half the time I think we have left together.

Except Cathy won't give us a time frame..

You might choose to go on a ventilator, which would give you more time.

If you can walk and still use your arms, you might want that.

If you call that living.

Hiss Hiss Hiss

For now, Harvey gets the BiPAP instead. A toaster-sized breathing machine, pushing air in, sucking it out.

It's like those cups that airplanes have in case of loss of cabin pressure.

You'll get more oxygen and feel better.

But no peanuts! And I don't get to go anywhere.

Pant, pant!

Cathy explains that for Harvey, every day is like climbing Mt. Everest. That's how little oxygen he's getting.

I'm overwhelmed, in a state of shock. And Harvey's making jokes?

When we get home, I throw together a late lunch. What I really want is a stiff drink.

Harvey is healthy one day.

Dying the next.

One of the things the speech pathologist taught was not to talk and eat at the same time.

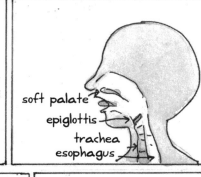

soft palate
epiglottis
trachea
esophagus

Those tiny adjustments the tongue and throat make so we don't breathe in our food are things Harvey has to actively focus on now.

It takes a while for Harvey to gag down his sandwich.

Can we talk about today?

Nothing to talk about.

Drinking is easier with a straw.

Has he weakened that much or am I just more aware of it all?

Why is he so stooped over? Is his neck okay?

It's a relief to get out of the house.

I'm picking up the kids from school.

Now Harvey's ready to talk.

Will you tell them why?

I'm thinking of taking a medical leave for the rest of the year.

It's none of their damn business. I can still teach. I just need time to figure out how to use a speech computer. Like the kind Stephen Hawking uses.

Will there be a next year?

There's only one place, one hour each day, where I can escape — the pool.
I swim with a master's team early every morning when it's still dark outside.

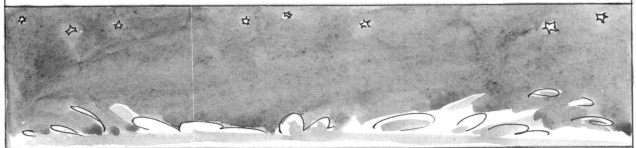

I love the stillness, the cold glitter of the stars, and when I cry, no one notices.
What's another drop among so many?

As Harvey loses muscles,
I rely on mine.

I don't think.

Ten 100s on
the 1:20.

You lead.

I just move and breathe.

It's almost Hanukkah now.
Harvey pretends everything is normal.
He works on his book.

Daddy?

But he can't look at the
boys any more than he
can look at me.

We have to tell
them. They know
something's wrong.

I've never seen him so furious.

NO!

My sons,
my disease!

But it's not his disease. It's rotting away at all of us.
First it killed our marriage. Now it's destroying our family.
And then Harvey will die. What will be left of us?

I hate to push Harvey, to take away the little control he has now.

How about when your sister comes? They'll wonder why she's here.

Helen never comes for Hanukkah and she was just here for the bar mitzvah.

I don't recognize this **man** anymore.

Fine! But *I'll* tell them after Helen gets here. *Not* before.

What a nice Hanukkah present.

The boys *do* know. Asa has a perpetually wary look to his face.

Why are you and Daddy always fighting?

People fight — like you and your brothers. It doesn't mean you don't love each other.

But I don't say those magic mom words: "Everything will be fine."

Does he notice?

I had another bad dream. There was a monster in the house!

Helen arrives as we're falling apart. She and Harvey have always been close, talking every Sunday. Maybe he'll open up to her.

Harvey?

He doesn't. Not to her, not to anyone.

Dad, is there a reason Aunt Pahu is here?

Dad?

We'll talk later.

It takes every ounce of self-control I have, but I don't nag. I don't say anything. Maybe the silence speaks louder than words.

Harvey takes Simon for a walk in the park behind our house.

When they come back, Simon looks like he's carved in granite.

He shuts me out, just like his father does.

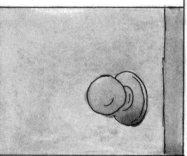

I want to hug him, to kiss the hurt and make it all better.

I know Dad has ALS. Can we *not* talk about it?

Next, it's Elias' turn. Then Asa's.

At least I can hug Elias.

I'm glad Dad told me. I knew something was wrong.

I thought he'd keel over when he was driving us to school. I was ready to grab the steering wheel and pull up the emergency brake if I had to.

But who will teach Asa to ride a bike or tie his shoe?

I guess Simon and I have to do it.

I tell him I can do those things, they're not his responsibility. But he's telling me I can't take Harvey's place. And he's right. I can't.

What can 6-year-old Asa understand?

Who is Lou Gehrig and why does Dad have his disease?

Fortunately, I have a large collection of children's books, including David Adler's *Lou Gehrig, the Luckiest Man.*

I get it — they put away Lou Gehrig's uniform so no one would get his germs.

It's like a kick in the gut. I had no idea Asa might worry he could catch this horrible disease.

No, they put away his uniform out of respect. Because he was such a good player, nobody could wear the same number. You know, it's not the kind of disease you get from germs. It just happens.

I can see Asa thinking hard. Maybe my answer is even scarier. Bad things happen for no reason at all. No way to prevent them.

Harvey didn't tell Asa he's dying, just that he's sick and won't ever get better.

Dad's like the luckiest man. Can we read it again?

The boys all know now, so we can tell them the truth when we go to our first ALS support group that weekend.

WELCOME A.L.S. SUPPORT GROUP

MEETING ROOM 301

It's not at a hotel, despite the conventioneer look of the sign greeting us at the hospital. Harvey's sister, Helen, comes with us, so we can all see what lies ahead.

MY NAME IS

It's a small club, one we don't want to belong to.

People take turns telling when they first realized something was wrong, when they were diagnosed, what challenges they're currently facing. There are four other people with Bulbar ALS like Harvey.

Trisha — diagnosed two years ago. She now only has the use of two fingers and a lot of spirit.

I TALK LIKE THIS

She'll die before the next month's meeting.

Caroline — diagnosed eighteen months ago, with no mobility at all now. She's locked in her body, able only to blink.

She'll also die before the January meeting.

David — like Harvey, recently diagnosed, the only other person with children at home, two teenage daughters.

I want to go hang gliding, before I can't.

He'll die six months after Harvey, but he gets to hang glide first.

Carl — diagnosed a year ago. He can still walk and talk, but swallowing has become almost impossible.

I brought a little show and tell today.

He speaks with that distinctive ALS slur.

He twirls his new gastric tube as if he's doing a striptease, clearly pleased with his new toy.

Ba—da— da—DA, da—da— da—DUM!

Insert formula here, to feed directly into the stomach.

He'll die four months after Harvey.

We hear a lot about wheelchair accessibility issues, feeding tubes, computers that speak for you, but nothing about ventilators. That's a line nobody wants to cross.

A gastric tube is one thing, a ventilator another.

That's when I'll call it quits.

A ventilator means 'round-the-clock nurses. We'd go bankrupt.

Harvey looks healthier than these people, but his breathing is so **bad**, he's actually worse. There will be no question of a wheelchair if we don't deal with the ventilator first.

It's too much for us to take in. The drive home is eerily quiet.

The kids don't ask, and we don't tell them anything about the support group.

Bye . . .

Helen leaves the next day, without really talking.

And Harvey won't talk to me.

Is there someplace you want to go? Something you've always wanted to do?

No! I just want to finish the book!

I thought we'd have one last trip together, some way of making the most of the time we have left. But it's already too late.

Because you're not aware of last things.

I don't think of our last kiss, our last "I love you," because I assume there will be others. We remember "firsts," are aware of them by their very nature. But last things sneak up on you, slip away, unnoticed, unmarked, unless they're part of big ritual events, like graduation, moving, divorce, going off to war.

Harvey and I share a lot of "lasts" and we don't even know it.

I thought Harvey and I would grow even closer, united in fighting the dread disease. Isn't that what's supposed to happen? Illness brings clarity of purpose and vision, weeding out the superficial, the trivial.

Isn't that what's supposed to happen?

Instead, Harvey focuses on himself, his work. I can feel him turn to stone whenever I reach out to touch him.

I'm not caught up in a gauzy made-for-TV special where people become noble and wise in the face of catastrophe.

I don't feel more spiritual, either. I don't even feel like a better person, truly appreciating life.

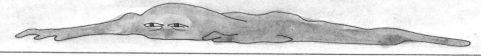

I feel like a wet rag. Exhausted. Used up. Hollowed out. There's nothing left to me at all.

This isn't how it's supposed to be.

The black fog of secrecy has lifted. We should be enjoying the clear air, the bright sunlight, the sparkling view of San Francisco from our window.

So why aren't we? When will things go back to the way they were? Or better even? All those stories about how emotionally deep and rewarding facing death can be — why isn't that *our* story?

Instead, it's laundry and shopping and errands, packing lunches and helping with homework. Nothing the least bit noble or enlightening.

Mom, there's no pickles.

Or apples. Or anything.

We can't snack on condiments!

This is the month to decide — to go on the ventilator or not. Harvey's breathing is so impaired, Cathy, the neurologist at the ALS Clinic, says we can't wait any longer. She gives us material to look over as homework.

Tracheotomy is the surgery to have a hole cut in the throat. Tracheostomy is the hole itself.

Is there a special school for how to make informational pamphlets? They all have the same look, with the obligatory African American and Asian. Where's the token Jew? The turbaned Sikh?

Who cares about the pictures? It's gross! Look, the woman has to write out what she wants to say.

Dad won't be able to talk?!

Isn't breathing more important? Harvey could talk using a computer like the women in the ALS support group. Or he could learn to speak on the exhale the way Christopher Reeve did after his accident left him dependent on a ventilator.

Is that our future?

The pamphlet is one thing, but the video seems too real, too horrible for the boys. I send them to Shelah's while we watch it.

We need to make this decision without distractions.

Ventilation is a serious choice . . .

Ed is totally paralyzed now. We have nurses to help, but they're expensive. Tens of thousands of dollars a month.

We've gone through our savings. I guess we have to sell the house now.

The ventilator is my friend.

I live in this nice facility with all the help I need.

They take good care of me.

A facility?

Nurses?

Bankruptcy?

I . . . I can't do it. I'm a terrible person, but I can't. How can I take care of you, the boys, and still write?

I don't want you to. Those people in the video are all paralyzed. I can still take care of myself, even on a ventilator.

Call those names Cathy gave you, the people who have spouses on a ventilator. Ask exactly what's involved.

I love Harvey. I can't imagine life without him. But I can't imagine being a caregiver, either. If I can't write or draw, I'll disappear. I can't think about it.

Stroke, stroke, stroke, breathe. Don't think. Don't feel. Just stroke, stroke, stroke, breathe.

Here are my questions. Ask *all* of them.

Harvey wants to know if he'll be in pain, if he'll be able to eat, drink, sleep, have a bowel movement. Will he have to wear diapers? That's his biggest concern. I want to know the risks, what needs to be done, and can I do it?

Harvey already walks stooped over, his neck too weak to hold up his head.

The first voice that answers is frail and gravelly.

Hello. Cathy from the ALS Clinic gave me your name. . .

Life on a ventilator? Well. . .I can't ever leave my husband, so there's that. Things are always breaking. Plus, his lungs need suctioning often.

So I stay awake nights to make sure he's okay. Our son comes a few hours every day so I can get some sleep. And a friend drops by once a week so I can get groceries.

But how do you earn a living?

We both took early retirement so I could be home full time.

It doesn't sound like caregiving. It sounds like prison.

A man answers the next call, but the situation is eerily similar, the voice equally drained.

Some nights I need to suction her lungs every fifteen minutes . . . it's exhausting . . .

Cathy hadn't said anything about suctioning. Nor had the informational pamphlet or video.

All that drainage that goes down your sinuses ends up in your lungs, just like you're continuously swallowing saliva without thinking about it.

With ALS, the muscles don't work to push things down, so secretions build up. You've got to get rid of them somehow or they'll clog up the lungs. That means suctioning.

How can you tell when she needs suctioning?

And what is suctioning?

Her breathing gets worse. Or the alarm goes off on the ventilator.

I have to insert a tube down the trach hole into the lungs and suction up all the gunk — quickly, though, because she can't breathe while I suction.

Could I do that? Be responsible for Harvey breathing or dying? How would I take care of the boys? There is still one more call to make. Can the news get any worse?

This time, the voice that answers is firm, energetic.

You can do this! I run my own business and I can still take care of Linda. The key is nurses. You have to get nurses.

Don't they cost a fortune?

Look at your insurance policy. They may be covered as a medical necessity. The problem is, there's a nursing shortage, so we don't have help every day. But we usually manage five days a week.

Just make sure you get one of those new laptop ventilators. They're light, so your husband can carry it wherever he goes. He's still walking, right?

I don't tell Harvey about the trapped, tired spouses. I tell him about portable ventilators and suctioning. I tell him that with nurses we can do this. And that luckily our insurance covers them.

I could suction myself, couldn't I?

My hands and arms are fine. We don't need nurses.

But when your arms get weak, then we can get nurses.

No, then it's time to pull the plug.

I know Harvey will get weaker, but I hope that the ventilator will buy us some time. And with more oxygen, life might be better for him.

In some ways, I'm right. In others, I couldn't be more wrong.

The spring semester will soon start and Harvey tires so easily, his speech is so slurred, how can he teach?

Have you told the art history department about the diagnosis?

No! They don't need to know. But I did apply for a medical disability leave for the spring semester.

I want to teach in the fall. I can lecture using a computer voice. If I tell them I have ALS, they'll get rid of me.

Why is there so much shame, so much stigma attached to horrible diseases? As if it's our fault if we get them.

I understand not telling the university about the ALS, but shouldn't we let the boys' school know?

No! I don't want my teacher to know!

Why does anyone need to know?

Go ahead, tell the school. I told the department.

It was the only way I could get them to give me the accommodation I'll need to teach in the fall. They didn't exactly ooze warmth and supportiveness.

Harvey has been a tenured professor for twenty years. He's been chair of the department, served on endless committees on all levels of the university. He deserves better.

Asa? I'm off the phone now!

Asa?

Asa?

Asa?

All my friends say the same thing.

Get your boys into therapy!

You should all be in therapy!

I find therapists who specialize in grief for all of us, except Harvey, who refuses.

I'm fine.

Simon won't talk.

It's okay.

Nor will Elias.

Can we play? This is a good game!

LIFE

I thought I wanted to talk . . .

So what exactly are your fears?

You're worried that your husband will die in front of you?

Hmmmm, so you're feeling stressed?

In front of your children?

Are things hard at home?

What I want to scream:

YES! MY HUSBAND IS DYING!

But instead I say, "Thanks, good bye." What else *could* I say? At least Asa has a good therapist.

41

Do the boys understand what's happening to us?
Is it better for them to know or not know?
How do you make a father's dying easier for a child?
I have no answers, no idea what to do.
And Harvey won't help. Or maybe he can't.

Asa, 6

Elias, 10

Simon, 13

Why does Asa look so wary all the time now?

Does Daddy love me?

Elias is angry with everyone except his father. He's very sweet to Harvey, oddly angelic.

No! NO!!

And Simon is a tightly shut door.

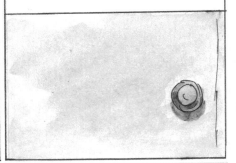

So what do I do? What can I do?

I look at family albums, nostalgic for the family we were. And aren't anymore. Harvey was so good at living, I thought he'd be good at dying, be present for us the same way. But it's not the same at all.

Bath time, which used to be special Daddy time, is my job now.

You know, Dad loves you very much even if he doesn't show it.

You have to remember back to how Dad was before he got sick and know that's how he really feels. When people are really, really sick, they think only about themselves.

I know. I don't care anyway.

Simon sees how it matters.

So does Elias.

Asa, want to play with my chess set? The one Aunt Debbie brought back from Poland?

You never let me touch that!

Sure you can!

Really?!

I feel worst for Asa about Dad being sick.

Why?

Because Dad won't be able to do with him all the things he did with Simon and me. Who's going to explain all that science stuff at the Exploratorium?

Simon and I will have to do it.

Elias is the loyalist. Every day after school, he makes a point of telling Harvey about his day.

Uh huh.

We're starting our California mission project and I'm . . .

Simon avoids his father as much as he can. As if by not seeing how weak Harvey has become, he can pretend nothing has changed. Until he can't.

HAND ME THE REMOTE.

SIMON! SIMON!

What?! Why can't you talk clearly? I can't understand you!

Mom!! Dad's talking and I don't know what he's saying!

Speech is hard for Harvey. Eating is worse. His jaw muscles no longer close, so his mouth hangs slackly open. Chewing is difficult. What's even harder is using his tongue to push the food to the back of his throat. A motion we don't even think about takes intense, deliberate effort.

Eeewww! Dad, that's gross!

I'm done . . .

HAKKGAKK GAKKK!

Pretty good meatloaf, Mom.

May I be excused?

Why did you let them leave? Family dinners are important!

But eating is even more important. I start allowing the boys a TV dinner before Harvey sits down at the table, so they can be out of earshot while he works on his food.

HACKKK! HAKKK! GAGG!

45

Shabbat is the one exception. But I give the boys a hearty snack before lighting the candles.

And I eat with Harvey — or try to.
His choking is hard to bear, a hoarse hacking of drowning on food.
I force myself to swallow, my tongue heavy in my mouth.

47

Until his cousin Liisa makes Asa a bracelet of paperclips.

This will keep the nightmares away.

Really?

Magically, the bracelet works. But paperclips break apart easily, so we change to beads. Still, we go through dozens.

Until Asa makes his own bracelet, his favorite.

This one lasts for years. All the way until Asa's own bar mitzvah . . .

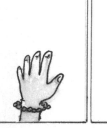

. . . when it finally breaks. It's chosen the right moment.

Harvey doesn't notice the bracelets. Or the nightmares.

But then, he has his own nightmare, the one where every day he wakes up to a little less of himself.

Me, I don't dream at all.
I throw myself into my next book.

But for the first time ever, Harvey doesn't look over the finished art when I'm done.

Can you take a look?

NOT NOW.

MAYBE LATER.

LATER, I SAID.

There is no later. The box of art gets sent out.
Another last thing I didn't notice go by.

The last time Harvey reads my work.

This is really funny!

The only thing that stays the same is the routine of swimming.
Every morning, I leave for the pool while the house is still asleep.
Harvey sleeps later than the boys now. His breathing is so labored,
I'm afraid he'll simply stop during the night.
Or I'll come back from the pool . . .

. . . and find he's died.

Each morning, I feel a surge
of relief when I get home.

Who ate all
the Cheerios?

Make toast
instead!

Where are
my socks?

Still I make myself swim. I need to.

I push away the worries, the fear, and throw myself into the water.
And for an hour, there's no more sickness. No more death. Just the water holding me.

By early February, Cathy insists it's time for the ventilator.
Harvey's face gets stonier with each sentence.

You wouldn't always be hooked up to it, but you could use it for longer periods than the BiPAP. And if you wait much longer, it will be emergency surgery. You don't want to pass out and have Marissa find you like that.

The pulmonologist, Dr. Barstow, says the opposite.

You don't want to become dependent on a machine.

Why not try a non-invasive ventilator first? You don't need a trach, just suck on a straw to breathe.

Harvey is his first ALS patient.

Of course, Harvey chooses the non-trach machine. The ventilator is delivered the next week.

GASP!

IT'S NOT WORKING.

CALL DR. BARSTOW.

GASP!

Simon, watch your brothers. I need to take Dad to the doctor.

An hour later, we're on the way to the E.R. where Dr. Barstow will meet us.

You know things are bad when you don't have to wait in the E.R., but are ushered right in.

You need to use muscles, or you lose them.

If Harvey gets the trach, his lungs will get lazy.

They'll depend on the ventilator.

Doesn't ALS reduce muscle control anyway?

LISTEN TO DR. BARSTOW!

Nothing has changed. Harvey still struggles to get enough air. But I don't mention the trach again. It has to be his choice.

Is Dad okay? You didn't say good bye when you left. You just left.

We all need a break, but Harvey can't go anywhere. There will be no last trips together.

Still, the boys can get away. My brother Steven offers to take them skiing in Tahoe with his family.

Come with us, Asa!

It'll be fun!

Sara would love for all her cousins to come.

No, I can't go.

Bye!

Bye!

Have fun.

What can I do to make things okay when they aren't?

You know, Dad's friends, Anne and Peter, are coming all the way from New York to visit this weekend. Maybe they can stay with Dad while I take you to the park or the science museum. Your choice.

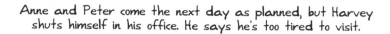
Anne and Peter come the next day as planned, but Harvey shuts himself in his office. He says he's too tired to visit.

He didn't tell us how bad he is. We should have come sooner.

He made it sound almost minor.

I don't know what he's telling people. He won't talk to me about anything.

Maybe he'll feel better tonight. I thought he might confide in you, you're so close.

But dinner is worse. I warned about the choking and that Harvey can't eat and talk at the same time. His muscles can't adjust quickly from speaking to swallowing.

I forget how hard it is to understand Harvey. I'm used to that distinctive ALS rale.

I'M SO TIRED. GOOD NIGHT.

It feels like it's already too late for anything.

No last good talk?

No last hug from Harvey even?

Is there any chance the trach would help? The ventilator?

I don't have the answers. As usual.

I was hoping you could stay with him while I take Asa to the park tomorrow. Just for an hour.

54

But the next morning, Harvey's much worse and the ventilator doesn't help.

CALL CATHY.

I CAN'T BREATHE.

Get Harvey to the hospital here. He needs the trach now! We'll schedule it as soon as we can, but that may be a few days and he should be where we can watch him.

Harvey agrees, which means he's scared.

Cathy gives detailed instructions on what to pack, what to expect. She says Harvey only has to be in the ICU for a couple of weeks after the surgery, which sounds quick. When I talked to the caregivers of people on ventilators, one had stayed in the hospital for nine months after getting the trach, the others for a month or two.

Are we going to the park?

I forgot about Asa. What kind of mother does that?

Luckily Anne and Peter come as soon as I call them. To watch Asa, though, not his dad.

How about we take you to the park? I'd love to see it!

You don't know where it is. It's secret!

I tell Asa I have to take Daddy to the hospital. I promise we'll get our park time another day. I wonder when.

Harvey hugs Asa good bye so tightly, it scares him.

Daddy hasn't hugged me in a long time. Why is he hugging me now?

How can I answer that?

GO HOME NOW. YOU CAN COME BACK TOMORROW. SURGERY WON'T HAPPEN FOR A FEW DAYS.

At the hospital, Harvey pushes me away. We both know this is a dividing line, but I've already lost my best friend and husband. Am I just a caregiver now?

You know how the car is a good place to sing your heart out? Turns out it's also the perfect place to cry.

I try to look normal by the time I get home.

Except, what's normal?

Asa, at least, has had a good weekend.
He's fallen in love with Peter.

We played cards and got pizza and went to three parks and got ice cream and read books . . .

We had a great time! We wish we could stay longer.

Bye, Asa. See you soon!

Simon calls on the way home from Tahoe. They've had a great time, too.

Elias crashed right into a guy —

it was just like a cartoon!

He sounds so happy, I hate to tell him about Harvey. But I do.

Oh.

Let me talk! Halloooooo!

Did Simon tell you how much syrup we put on our pancakes? We made syrup soup!

Nice, I say. Then I give Elias the news.

Why didn't you call us?!

I didn't want to ruin your vacation. Are you mad at me?

Is it better you didn't know or worse?

Better.

I guess.

CLICK

Once they get home, they act like regular kids.

Was it fun?

You should have come!

We made a snowman!

I try to keep things normal, taking the boys to school, then rushing to the hospital to be with Harvey, whether he wants me there or not. I bring him *The New York Times*, fresh fruit and cookies, then hurry back to get the boys from school. I throw together a quick dinner, rush to the grocery store, do laundry, pack school lunches. Everything else gets cancelled — guitar and piano lessons, Hebrew school.

Spaghetti again?

I like spaghetti!

There's one more thing to cancel. I signed up to be a parent helper for Asa's first grade Valentine's Day party. But that will be the day after Harvey's surgery.

You promised!

I can still bring cupcakes, napkins, lemonade. I just can't stay to help with the art project. I'm really sorry, but something has come up. Thanks for understanding.

You haven't come to my class *once*! Sonya's mom has come twice. So has Jamal's dad. Not you!

I'm sorry, but Dad needs me with him. You can still pass out the cupcakes. You can even pick them out at the store. I'll come to your class another day and do a super fun art project.

Asa, does this really matter so much to you?

Yes! It's important! Very important!

Please, Asa

How about we read a book?

Will Asa ever forgive me? Will Harvey?

The next day . . .

DON'T COME BEFORE THE SURGERY TOMORROW.

I NEED TO BE ALONE, OKAY? COME AFTER. THAT'S WHEN I'LL NEED YOU.

I'm both hurt and relieved. I desperately want to be close to Harvey. And I dread it.

It's hard to leave, knowing the next time I see him, he'll have a hole in his throat. So Harvey turns on the TV, his way of shooing me out.

I love you.

I'll always love you.

I want to curl up in the narrow hospital bed with him. Instead, I back out of the room, holding Harvey in my sight as long as I can.

The time spent in traffic is a relief, a chance to think about who Harvey was and to mourn what's already gone.

Firsts:

Our first trip to New York together, Harvey drove through Long Island so we could arrive by ferry. My first view of the city is the way my grandparents would have seen it when they came to this country.

Our first year of marriage, living in Paris, seeing every major cathedral and abbey in France. Walking the labyrinth at Chartres.

You like the warm water, don't you, cutie?

With Asa

With Simon

Lemme!

With Elias

My face feels puffy with tears by the time I get the boys from school.

Cupcakes!

Normally, I would steer Asa toward healthier muffins, like the school prefers. But he knows I owe him.

I pick these!

The next morning, I walk with Asa to class.

Have a fun party! Remember Aunt Shelah is picking you up today so I can stay with Dad.

I know, I know.

Finally, Erin, the ALS respiratory therapist, walks in.

Is he okay? Can I see him?

He's fine. But unfortunately there isn't a free bed in the ICU yet, so he's still in recovery.

Can I see him there?

Harvey's already in surgery by the time I get there. I'm directed to a waiting room where I wait. And wait. And wait.

SUPPORT GROUP FOR FAMILIES BRAI

She'll be off the ventilator soon.

WANT TO KNOW ABOUT BRAIN CANCER TOP TEN QUESTIONS:

Why is it taking so long? Has something gone wrong?

Erin explains that normally visitors aren't allowed in recovery, but Harvey's very anxious to see me and it could be hours before he's moved. She'll let me in as long as I promise to "be discreet." Meaning, I guess, don't stare.

The recovery room isn't the quiet, drowsy place I imagined, but noisy and busy, crackling with activity.

See, the first thing he did was ask for you.

MY WIFE?

With the trach in now, Harvey can't talk.

It's a shock to see him. I expected a clean tube, like in the trach pamphlet. Instead, there's a bloody wound, as if Harvey was shot in the throat.

The trach has been stitched onto the skin to hold it in place.

Harvey takes my hand tightly. I can feel how terrified he is.

For the first time since the diagnosis, all the walls of anger and denial fall away.
What's left is need, fear, and love. Even without being able to talk, Harvey's more
open, more nakedly present than he's been in months. I'm as scared as he is,
a deep terror clawing at my stomach. But I can bear it. I can bear it all.
So long as he lets me in like this, takes me with him on this last horrible journey.

Erin leaves. The nurses change shifts. It's after 8 pm and Harvey is still in the recovery room. I don't want to leave him, to break the magic spell of his presence, but I haven't checked in with Shelah. I don't know how long she can stay with the boys.

I'm not going anywhere. I just need to call Shelah and ask if she can spend the night.

I go out in the hall to use my phone.

I have to work early tomorrow. You should come home. You need to sleep, too. How can you help Harvey if you're up all night?

She's right, but it's so hard to leave now that I have Harvey back.

Shelah can't stay, but I promise I won't go until you've fallen asleep. I'll come back tomorrow as soon as I can. You'll probably still be asleep.

The nurse notches up the Ativan drip and Harvey finally relaxes. I'm moved by the nurse's gentle care, the way he touches Harvey. I'm leaving him in good hands, with someone who's a natural caregiver.

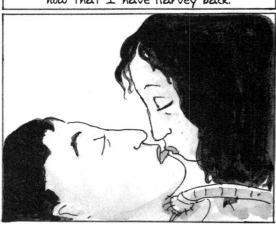

Harvey's breathing slows, his face a mask of calm. I kiss him and tear myself away. The connection is so profound, I feel like I'm leaving part of myself behind.

After the close intensity of the recovery room, the fresh night air is a jolting relief. I walk to my car, bone-tired, but keenly aware of my own strong legs. I take deep, deep breaths.

The next morning, I assure the boys their dad is fine, then hurry them to get to school early.

I want to get to San Francisco before Dad wakes up.

Okay, okay.

For once, the traffic isn't bad, and I pull into the garage before nine. I'm too impatient for the notoriously slow elevators, so I run up the stairs to the eighth floor, where the ICU is.

Harvey looks pale and gaunt and shrunken, but he's still asleep. One small victory.

He's still asleep when Erin pulls me outside.

Yesterday was hard, but the main thing is he's breathing fine now. Once he gets used to the ventilator, he should have a lot more energy. You'll see.

Erin has already talked to our insurance case manager and the home health company about getting Harvey a laptop ventilator. Most people using ventilators are in wheelchairs, so weight doesn't matter. For Harvey, who can still walk, it matters a lot.

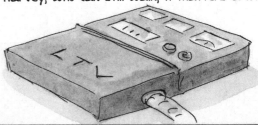

He really waited until the last minute to get the trach. If he'd done this last month, he could have gone on and off of the ventilator. Now his lung muscles are so weak, he may be on the ventilator twenty-four hours a day. It's important we get him a light one, something he can carry himself.

I know Erin's trying to be helpful, but it feels like she's blaming Harvey.

It's only been two and a half months since the diagnosis!

Most people take a year to deal with that news. Harvey didn't even have time for that before having to decide about the trach!

It was too much for him to handle at once. Too much for me.

When Harvey wakes up, his eyes search for me. He smiles, the first smile in a long time.

Your Tracheostomy

Before Harvey can leave the hospital, I need to be able to clean the trach and replace the inner canula, which goes inside the trach and needs changing daily.

Here's what the trach pamphlet and the ventilator video both failed to mention, but all the caregivers warned me about: suctioning.

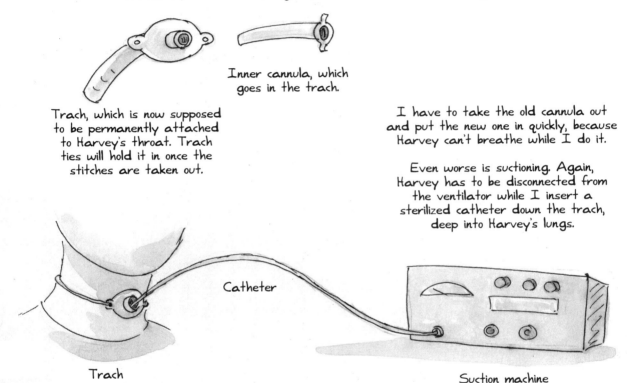

Inner cannula, which goes in the trach.

Trach, which is now supposed to be permanently attached to Harvey's throat. Trach ties will hold it in once the stitches are taken out.

I have to take the old cannula out and put the new one in quickly, because Harvey can't breathe while I do it.

Even worse is suctioning. Again, Harvey has to be disconnected from the ventilator while I insert a sterilized catheter down the trach, deep into Harvey's lungs.

Catheter

Trach

Suction machine

One hand guides the catheter while the other controls the suction, starting it only as I bring the catheter slowly back up, *not* as it goes down.

So what could go wrong? Too deep and I'll tear the fragile membrane of Harvey's lungs. Same with if I switch on the suction at the wrong time. And if I don't insert the catheter far enough, the mucous will be left collecting in Harvey's lungs, choking him.

It's scary, especially since the signal for how far to go is when Harvey coughs and looks pained. I have to hurt him a little to help him a lot.

This is something Harvey thought he could do himself, but for now, I have to be his nurse.

The intimacy of the recovery room is gone, but we have a renewed sense of companionship, of working together as a team.

I'll pick up your mail at the university and bring it to you. Maybe you'll have enough energy now to teach in the fall.

It's always hard to leave, but my visiting hours are framed by when the boys are in school.

You're late again.

Did you forget about us?

I tell them I'm trying my best, but we all know I'm failing.

I'm hoping Harvey can come home soon, but it's complicated. The home health company has to provide the laptop ventilator, I have to prove I'm a competent caregiver, and a whole range of doctors have to approve his discharge. One specialist is Dr. Barstow, the pulmonologist.

I'm sorry, Harvey.

You were my first ALS patient and I didn't realize that ALS demands different treatment than the pulmonary diseases I usually see.

Harvey doesn't care about the apology, but I appreciate it. Harvey's too worried about his own test — he can't leave until he can swallow food down his esophagus, not his trachea.

Most terrifying of all, Erin's fear has come to pass. She tries taking Harvey off the ventilator, but he can't breathe on his own anymore. At all. His life depends on a machine.

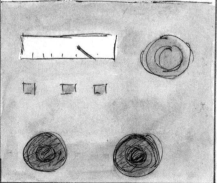

What happens if the ventilator breaks? If the power goes out? I thought the ventilator would give Harvey more freedom, but maybe that's an illusion.

I'm working on the LTV, the laptop ventilator, plus you'll need an extra battery while you drive Harvey home and in case of a power failure. As an extra precaution, you'll need an Ambu bag.

You just squeeze the bag manually to force air into Harvey's lungs. That'll work till you get help.

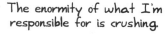
The enormity of what I'm responsible for is crushing.

And then I come home to the boys where even dinner is beyond me.

I need help!

Moooooooom!

I can't do this!

It's your homework, not mine! Do I have to go back to first grade all over again?

I feel like a total bitch. I take a deep breath, try to calm down and help Asa, but both of us are miserable.

Elias! How can you be so clumsy!

Oops!

This isn't me. I'm *not* like this. And who cares about spills when Harvey's dying?

I feel thin and easily torn, like a paper doll.

Not the strong support the boys need — or Harvey.

You're always tired and cranky. We never go anywhere. We never do anything fun.

I know. I'm sorry. I'm working on it.

I want life to be normal for them. I just don't know how.

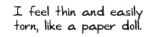

Still, I keep swimming, greedy for the hour in the water when I don't think, don't feel, just move.

I hold my breath as long as I can, kick my legs as hard as I can. I don't care about going fast. I just want to wear myself out, to feel that pleasant ache in my muscles.

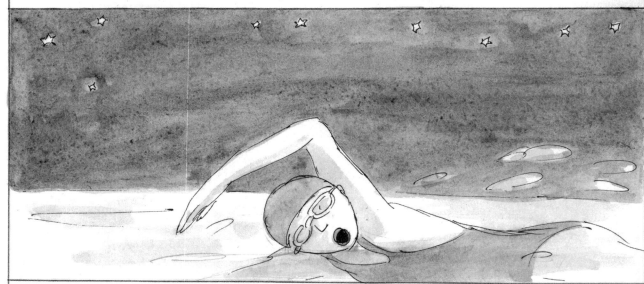

Now the boys are on their own in the morning with Simon in charge. They're dressed, fed, and ready to go to school by the time I get home from the pool. That's the new normal.

After a week in the ICU, Harvey learns how to eat with the trach. He can talk now, a word or two at a time. I miss the deep round timbre of his voice, but the harsh, whispery words still sound sweet.

Want to go home tomorrow?

YES!

Can he really go?

Cathy says it's time, but I have to clear it with half a dozen people, make an appointment to have the trach stitches taken out, meet with a nutritionist, speech pathologist, a social worker.

Everyone signs off except Optal, the home health care company. The LTV is ready, but not the external battery needed for the trip home.

It's a holiday weekend, President's Day. Optal wants Harvey to wait until Tuesday.

I WANT TO GO HOME! THE LTV BATTERY LASTS AN HOUR ~ THAT'S ENOUGH.

Unless there's a traffic jam . . .

We need a towering pile of supplies, but as I argue with Optal, I realize the battery is just an excuse. The holiday weekend is the real reason. They'll be understaffed and don't want to risk responding too slowly if there are problems with the LTV.

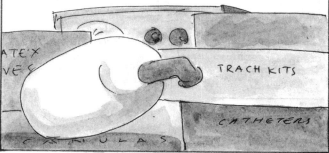

I should relish the extra days in the hospital because that means nurses are caring for Harvey, not me. They're the ones awake with him at night, suctioning his lungs every few hours.

Except I want him home. I want him to have his life back, to be with his sons, to work on his book. I should be terrified of the enormous responsibility of being a caregiver. But I just want my husband home.

It's discharge day at last. I corral Steven into helping me since I'm not sure how to handle Harvey and the ventilator at once.

I'll run up and get Harvey. You wait with the car.

Okey dokey.

I run up to the eighth floor for the last time. Whatever lies ahead has to be better than the no-man's-land of the ICU.

Harvey's dressed and ready to go. He's aged years in these last weeks and lost so much weight, I had to punch a new hole in his belt. His once thick black hair is thin and brittle now, washed-out like the rest of him.

A nurse helps me get him with the wheelchair.

You go ahead to the car. I have to stop at the nurse's station.

We need all this?

No sign of Steven, just a cop who has no idea what a ventilator is.

Harvey pushes himself upright, standing weakly in the thin February light. I'd say it's his first taste of fresh air in weeks except there's no more fresh air for him. Only ventilator air.

School is off for the week, so the boys are home. I've warned them that Harvey's thinner, weaker, and has a hole in his throat, but really, how can I prepare them?

Harvey settles into his office while Steve and I put away the supplies.

Harvey writes on the clipboard he now carries everywhere.

"Would you rather I talk to you like this?"—

That's worse! Gotta go!

Elias and Simon at least give their dad stiff hugs. Then they escape as well.

It's a lot for the boys to get used to. Really, they're glad for you to be home. Just give them time.

Steven brings in the last of the supplies and then he's gone, too. We're left alone with our new reality.

Harvey wants to wash off the hospital smell, but a shower means disconnecting from the ventilator. He rejects the stool I stick in the shower as something for an invalid. He stubbornly stands while I wait for him to fall.

After several seconds, the ventilator alarm goes off, signaling a disconnect. I'm definitely disconnected.

Clean, dry, dressed, Harvey can walk around the house, but he's so weak, he leans on the ventilator, slotted into its rolling stand. It's like a walker for him, though he'd never admit to that.

Going up the short flight of stairs to his office, however, is tricky. I have to walk behind him, carrying the ventilator. If I get too far away, the ventilator tubing tugs on Harvey. Any further and I risk pulling out the trach. It's an awkward dance, one Harvey resents sharing with me.

Back in his office, Harvey turns on his computer, shutting me out again.

The Book

Our new routine is this: after I take the boys to school, I help
Harvey upstairs so he can work on his book, the one he worked
on in Rome, the one he's worked on our entire marriage.

The psalter of Saint Louis is one of France's national treasures.
It's so highly prized, very few scholars have had the privilege
of seeing it. Harvey is one of those scholars.

The prayer book is full of Old Testament stories, but what
interests Harvey most is the choices Louis made, the stories
he included, the interpretation he gave them. That and the
incredibly high quality of the painting, expressive of a
new courtly elegance.

I want to ask if there's a colleague who can finish the book if Harvey doesn't. I want to ask about our finances, life insurance, college savings.

Whenever I try, Harvey cuts me off. I don't even know how much money we have in savings in the bank.

How could I let myself be so ignorant?

HONK!

Those first days at home, I can barely work myself. I bought Harvey a party horn to honk when he needs me and the demands are constant — suctioning every two hours, Ativan to calm him down, the newspaper, the mail, something to eat or drink.

Nights are just as bad. Suctioning is a 'round-the-clock job, as the caregivers had warned me.

Still, no matter how exhausted I am, as soon as Harvey can suction himself, I get up at 5 am to go swimming.

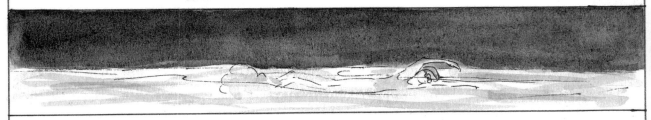

It's the only normal thing I have left.

I know I'm being selfish, that it's risky to leave Harvey alone.

HAVE A GOOD SWIM?

Yes!

Harvey never once asks me to stay home. He knows how much I need to go.

That first weekend home, Harvey's brother and sister come to visit.

How is everyone?

So good to see y'all!

Uncle Sid!

Aunt Pahu!

The boys are eager to talk. Harvey isn't.

His speech is already so hard to understand. This is all happening too fast. I can't believe it's real.

Harvey won't let us help him, but we can do something for you.

Go out with some friends tonight. We'll have pizza with the boys.

Really?

I call two close friends, an author and a bookseller, and we arrange to meet at a nearby restaurant.

I won't be long and Sid has my cell number.

Kathleen and Jillian are already at the restaurant when I get there.

It's been way too long!

You need a break!

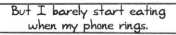 But I barely start eating when my phone rings.

 I'm sorry, but Harvey is having problems breathing. You have to come home.

 Sorry — another time!

Definitely!

 BEEP BEEP BEEP

I change the inner cannula, but it doesn't look clogged. I check the tubing on the ventilator.

Nothing.

Later that night, the alarm shrills. It takes me panicky seconds to figure out which tubing has broken and to switch it out, while Harvey pants, ashy still.

Helen and Sid leave the next day, but I'm not going anywhere.

I'm trapped, chained to the ventilator.

 This is as normal as we get now — me, folding laundry in the dining room while Harvey, Elias, and Asa watch *Star Trek*. Simon, as usual, hides in his room. But I have the feeling I've forgotten something.

Then I see the water seeping down the hall.

Elias' bath! I forgot all about it!

There's water all the way in Simon's room!

Poor Mom. You're so bad at life.

I can help!

We're out of towels!

Elias never takes a bath again. He showers instead.

Harvey seems oblivious to it all.

I wish I knew what he's thinking, feeling.

The List

Months later, I find a list Harvey made in early February, before getting the trach.

1) If I'm still ambulatory and can move and type and reach and do for myself, then having the trach & ventilator might be ok:
   - you could sleep w/Marissa, be with kids
   - you might have more energy, phys & intell
   - you might be able to speak, some
   - you might be able to work on book or even teach
   - what kind of requisite care and how pay for it?
   - impact of strangers in house and time it takes to hire people
   - impact on Marissa's work

2) eventually lose ability to swallow; will need tube. No taste. No restaurants, going out, meals together, but you don't eat. Impact on boys? How will boys talk to me, I to them?

3) eventually lose voice. How will boys talk to me, I to them? Synthesizer? Impact on boys? Will anyone want to study w/me if I speak thru a machine?

4) eventually lose mobility. Need many to help do everything. Wheelchair but so many split levels at home. How get around? Can't speak, eat, move, barely breathe, just being kept alive. Outrageous expensive. Not worth it.

So issues are:
1) Are you sure you can care for yourself with a ventilator? Does someone always have to be with me? Greater chance of respiratory diseases? More/less energy? What kind of mobility is there really?
2) Investigate talking machines now and record some things.
3) How stop respiration if have trach?

Clearly going downhill. What do? Only breathing getting worse BUT losing weight, etc., so other problems probably not far behind. If trach, then hospital and home with nurses and locked into a machine. UGHHHHH. But you can walk and take care of yourself? Can you? Even with your feeling so feeble? Is trach inevitable? Incredibly scary? End of this life? How connected are you? You've been getting remote, as though slowly cutting self off, preparing self for departure. Aren't there things you want to do, eg. travel, be with family, finish book, teach again? Not that teaching so important, but want to show that CAN DO IT, that not felled by this disease.

It breaks my heart to read it.
Maybe Harvey needs to be distant.
That's how he faces death.

Is dying like giving birth, something you have to do alone? With each child, the world fell away and there was only a huge elemental force coursing through me. It wasn't a hazy, romantic event. There was no sense of us as a couple, or even of me, as a person — just the power of something bigger. It was only after the baby slipped out and elation lifted us up that we came together as a couple again.

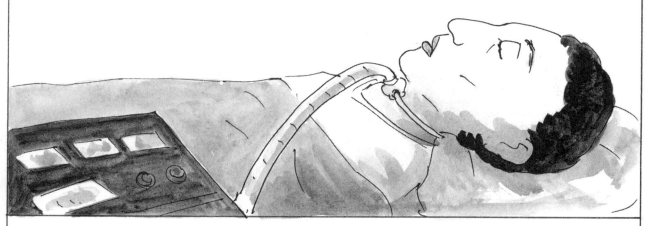

Is dying like that? Something that takes all your focus, all your concentration? A physical demand that strips away your sense of self?

Have I already lost Harvey to the process of dying?

We're told that major illness deepens us, makes us grateful for our lives. But for me, ALS doesn't work that way.

I'm not a bigger, nobler person and neither is Harvey.

There's always something medical to deal with. Now it's Harvey's feet. They've swollen so much, they hurt.

I'll take you to the clinic after I drop off the boys.

WE CAN JUST SEE MY DOCTOR HERE.

IN BERKELEY.

So no grocery shopping that day. Which means pasta for dinner again. I don't take Harvey to stores.

It's bad enough going to the doctor. I can practically hear what people are thinking, their stares are so loud.

I hope it's not contagious.

What's wrong with him?

What's that machine?

But Dr. Andrews is even worse.

Have you thought about hospice?

We don't need that yet!

Well, you have to expect people to be taken aback when they see you.

!?!

After a day on the diuretic, Harvey's feet are better, but his breathing is so strained, I take him to the E.R.

...CAN'T...

...BREATHE...

Even the ventilator isn't helping.

Harvey doesn't even try to talk.

Anyway, let me know when you're ready and I'll arrange everything.

The doctor gives us a push for hospice (no!) and a diagnosis of venous pooling, something that happens if you're in bed for long periods. Harvey needs to elevate his feet and take the diuretic the doctor prescribes.

At the E.R. . . .

It's the diuretic.

Someone on a ventilator should *never* take one. It dries up your secretions, so they're like concrete sticking to your lungs, blocking air flow.

At least this time I can take Harvey home with a nebulizer and a drug to moisten his lungs, but no more seeing doctors who don't know ALS. And pasta for dinner again.

I'm sorry I was so crabby with you today.

You're always crabby!

Poor Mom! She needs a vacation from all of us.

I feel less grumpy already. Must be your good night kisses.

What I really need are nurses. The nursing agency has assessed Harvey, insurance has approved them. We just need to find actual nurses.

Harvey hates the idea. He wants me to take care of him — even though I'm so bad at it.

The case manager recommends a night nurse so I can sleep. But I want one during the day so I can do things with the kids.

Bonnie will spend a day with you and see how she likes it. It has to be a good fit because having a nurse is like having a roommate.

I thought we'd be trying out the nurse . . .

. . . but she'll be trying out us. I lay out what we can offer her.

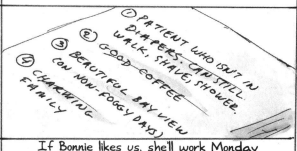

① PATIENT WHO ISN'T IN DIAPERS. CAN STILL WALK, SHAVE, SHOWER.
② GOOD COFFEE
③ BEAUTIFUL BAY VIEW (ON NON-FOGGY DAYS)
④ CHARMING FAMILY

If Bonnie likes us, she'll work Monday through Friday. Jean can come on Sunday. Saturday, we'll be on our own.

Bonnie comes early enough for me to take the boys to school. The boys won't look at her. Neither will Harvey.

We're so glad you're here! Help yourself to coffee, tea, anything. I'll be back soon

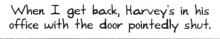
When I get back, Harvey's in his office with the door pointedly shut.

Is everything okay?

Oh yes, fine. Professor Stahl just asked that I stay outside. I won't check vitals or do trach care until he's ready.

It's hard for him to get used to needing help.

I understand.

Harvey is her first ALS patient. Her experience is with children on ventilators, which seems even more sad.

But I imagine children are more pliable.

LEAVE ME ALONE! YOU, TOD, MARISSA!

When Bonnie tries to suction him, Harvey grabs the catheter and does it himself, so angry that he tears the fragile lung tissue and suctions blood along with mucous.

After a couple of days, though, Harvey softens to Bonnie. Her familiar Texas twang helps. But he never forgives me. I've failed him. Profoundly.

Why are you always angry at me?

I'M NOT MAD AT YOU.

It feels like you're in the land of the very sick and you're shutting me out because I'm healthy.

DON'T BE RIDICULOUS. LET ME WORK. WE'LL TALK LATER.

But there is no later. We never talk about any of it.

I rely on my sister, Shelah, since I can't talk to Harvey.

He's acting like a teenager, picking fights. Only this separation isn't about leaving home. It's about leaving period. About dying.

He's a completely absent father now. I know it's because he feels he has nothing to offer the boys anymore, but that's idiotic. He could even email them if talking is too hard.

I'm sorry, Shelah, I'm ranting.

I hate my life right now.

Shelah reminds me of the same thing I tell the boys — Harvey does still love me. He just can't show it anymore.

Ave Mariaaaaaaa!

I finger memories like polished stones for comfort, calling them up to remind myself that yes, he loves me.

One of my favorites is my 40th birthday party, two years earlier. Harvey planned an elaborate surprise party. Most impressive — and typical of Harvey who never assumes something is impossible — he convinced a colleague's wife, a professional lieder singer, to bring her harpsichord to the restaurant and give a private recital. I was filled with the beauty of the music.

And gratitude that Harvey was mine, that he had created such an enchanting evening for me.

I try to give Asa the same kind of memories.

Here's when Dad built that sand castle with you in Hawaii.

This is when Dad was strong enough to carry me on my shoulders.

I remember that!

Asa finds his own way to connect with his father.

Like Harvey, who can't sip from a cup anymore, Asa only uses a straw now.

We buy a lot of straws. It becomes such a ritual that for years after Harvey's death, Asa still uses straws. Until I make him stop.

Elias and Asa often used to go with Harvey to his office on the weekends. They played on the outdated typewriter or looked through the pretty picture books, facsimiles of medieval manuscripts.

Even on the ventilator, Harvey goes to the office weekly. Not to work, but to pick up mail, books, files. Now we go early on Sunday, before the library housing his office officially opens. There's less chance then of running into colleagues and students. Neither of us want to face the uncomfortable stares. So far, just the two of us go, but I'm trying for a reconnection with the boys.

Do you want to come to Dad's office with us? It's been a long time since you've gone.

I'll stay. Asa can go.

Yes!

Yes!

Is the typewriter still there? Can I play with it?

Are there real bells in the campanile? When do they ring them? Maybe we can go up and see the view.

I bet it's pretty!

Emergency equipment, Ambu bag, tubing, catheters, suction machine, just in case.

What number do we need? I'll press the button! Let me!

Ding!

The stakes are high for Asa. He wants this visit to be like all the others before, a special treat where he's invited into his father's world.

Can I have the key? The key, Dad!

This is another cherished part of the routine, unlocking the office door.

Dad, please!

PLEASE!

PLEASE!!

How can Harvey ignore the naked pain in his child's voice?

Asa stands there, stunned, then turns and runs back down the hall.

I run after him, nauseous with grief, my heart a dead weight in my chest. Even now, so many years later, it's hard to write this.

Asa, I'm so sorry. Dad doesn't mean it. He still loves you! He just can't show it anymore.

I don't care.

The father he knew is gone. Instead, there's an ogre who pushes him away. I know just how he feels.

Now Asa won't even step into the office. He waits outside while Harvey collects what he wants.

You owe Asa an apology. You could have answered him.

Harvey shakes his head dismissively.

I notice that Harvey pushes himself up from the chair, too weak to get up otherwise. I watch for every nuance of physical change, wanting to be prepared, to keep him safe.

But the worst changes aren't the physical ones. Who is he becoming that he can be so cruel? Is it the self-absorption of dying or something else?

We drive home in silence. Harvey won't apologize. Asa won't talk. And I have no words to make things right.

The following September, back to school night, second grade. Asa's teacher warns me that the class has all done self-portraits and that his might be a "little disturbing."

It's a child's version of Munch's *The Scream.* The mother in me wants to crumple up on the floor, but the artist in me admires the emotional intensity Asa's managed in crayon.

It's a hard year for Asa. He's constantly running away — in an airport, in midtown Manhattan, in a jungle in Mexico where for ten terrified minutes, I imagine him drowned in a crocodile-filled lake or eaten by a jaguar.

Why do you keep running away?

You can't keep me safe. You couldn't save Dad.

Besides, if I die, I'll get to see Dad.

Asa's art teacher at his school offers to do art therapy with him. The first thing he makes is a clay skeleton.

Still, it's a step. He starts talking about death.

And when he's seven, he figures out his own way to reach Harvey.

To Dad, from Asa. Today is my birthday!

APRIL

I want to make things more normal for the boys. Now that we have nurses and Harvey's better at suctioning himself, it even seems safe to go out at night.

Sterile water, suction machine

So I ask if Harvey will be okay with Elias and Asa while I take Simon to his guitar lesson.

Or I can ask a friend to take him.

THAT'S RIDICULOUS. WE DON'T NEED HELP.

I'LL BE FINE. JUST LEAVE THE SUCTIONING EQUIPMENT NEAR ME.

I make sure Harvey has everything he needs. But the ventilator can always malfunction (it has twice before). I'm still taking a chance.

JUST GO ALREADY.

Emergency equipment

It's been so long since I've driven at night, it feels odd.

Does it bother you that Dad's on a ventilator?

Why should it bother me? I'm not the one with a hole in his throat.

It's okay. It keeps him alive.

If there are things you want to hear from Dad, you should email him — like if you want to know family stories . . .

Yeah, and about college. I want to know what advice he has.

Of course, Simon wants that. He's probably imagined how they would tour campuses, talking to his dad's friends and colleagues everywhere.

I can't do that for him.

I've brought something to read, but end up using the half-hour lesson time to cry.

Good lesson?

Yeah.

We drive home in silence.

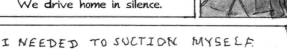

We're back! Everything okay?

WE ALMOST HAD A DISASTER.

I NEEDED TO SUCTION MYSELF. THERE WAS A LOT OF GUNK CLOGGING MY LUNGS.

BUT YOU FORGOT THE MIRROR.

How could I be so stupid?!

I'm so sorry!

What did you do?

I TRIED TO GET ELIAS' ATTENTION SO HE COULD BRING ME THE MIRROR, BUT HE DIDN'T HEAR ME.

ELIAS!

You weren't paying attention? How could you NOT hear that horn?!

The TV was loud. I didn't hear it.

FINALLY HE HEARD ME AND RAN TO GET THE MIRROR.

IT WAS A CLOSE THING, MARISSA.

I'm SO sorry! Next time, someone else can drive Simon.

I'm not gone for an hour and Harvey almost suffocates on his own secretions.

I could have come home to find Harvey dead, and it's all my fault.

IT ALL TURNED OUT OKAY.

Then I remember Elias.

How could I expect a child to care for someone on a ventilator?

Can I come in?

KNOCK FIRST— GET CLEARANCE, THEN ENTER CLEARANCE GIVEN ONLY BY ELIAS

Elias?

"Oh Elias, I'm so sorry."

"It wasn't your fault — it was mine! I shouldn't have yelled at you. I forgot the mirror, not you."

Elias nods, but I can tell he doesn't believe me.

I add it to my pile of guilt. I'm failing Harvey, Simon, Elias. And now Asa.

"Mom, I can't swallow. My throat is scratchy and clogged."

"I can't walk anymore. My legs are too weak."

"You can't catch Dad's disease. You're fine."

I'm still swimming early, proving to myself how strong my own legs are. No matter what, I'm swimming.

In fact, that's the only time I leave Harvey alone now, so when a meeting with booksellers is scheduled on an evening, I ask Bonnie if she'll stay late. She's fine with that.

"When will you be back?"

"I'll only be gone for an hour or so. I'll be home by eight, okay?"

"Eight. Eight o'clock."

I try to overestimate so Asa won't worry, but I don't wear a watch and it's only once I'm back in the car that I see it's 8:02.

"Sorry, Bonnie! I'll be there in twenty minutes!"

"No problem."

Asa!

ASA!

ASA!

whimper. . .

ASA!

You said eight o'clock!

I imagine Asa watching the minutes tick by. At 8:01, he thinks I'm gone forever. The reassuring truth he learned as a two-year-old, that your parents go away, but always come back, no longer holds true for him.

I can't make it right.

I'm so sorry.

I'm sorry.

I'm sorry.

There are no more normal days.
No more normal nights.

WHOOOOOOOO OOOOOOOSSSHH

There's only the ventilator.
And its constant swooshing sound.

I can never sleep with noisy air conditioners or heaters on. The ventilator is even worse.

By the middle of April, I give up. I tell Harvey I'm going to sleep in the living room. I'll hear him if he needs me, but I'll finally be able to sleep.

WHY CAN'T YOU SLEEP WITH ME? IT'S NOT NOISY AT ALL.

YOU CAN PRETEND IT'S THE SOUND OF THE OCEAN. VERY SOOTHING.

WE'RE SUPPOSED TO SLEEP TOGETHER.

Why are you making a bed on the sofa? You should sleep with Dad. He'll be all by himself.

If I could sleep with the noise of the ventilator, I would. I'll still take care of Dad.

What if Dad has nightmares?

Then I'll tuck him back in, like I do for you.

If only it were that easy . . .

We get used to the nurses, timing everything around their schedules, used to the ventilator, suctioning, and Harvey's demands. But there are limits.

Asa's friend, Aki, is coming over today.

ASA CAN GO TO HIS HOUSE. I DON'T WANT THEIR NOISE.

Three boys live here. You're sick, but they're not. So they need to have friends over.

I want to support Harvey. Maybe if he'd allowed me to share this last journey with him, I would choose differently.

But he doesn't, and I don't. I choose the boys. I can't help Harvey live, but I can help them.

Asa is excited coming home from school with his friend. He races Aki to the house.

That's my dad. He has a hole in his throat so he can breathe through that tube.

Okay.

Can Chloe sleep over tomorrow? We can watch movies in my room and stay up late, right?

Sure.

Chloe and Elias have been friends since they were babies. Now they love watching scary movies together. Harvey used to read bedtime stories to Chloe when she slept over, she came over so often.

Now he hates the idea of her coming over.

WHY ARE YOU DOING THIS TO ME? I'M EXHAUSTED BY THE END OF THE DAY. I NEED QUIET!

And Elias needs friends over. They'll be quiet, I promise.

YOU DON'T EVEN ASK IF IT'S ALRIGHT WITH ME. YOU JUST TELL ME.

THIS IS MY HOUSE, TOO!

YOU'RE SO HIGH-HANDED THESE DAYS. WHAT I WANT DOESN'T MATTER.

Of course it does.

I'm just trying to balance what's best for the boys with what's best for you.

Six months ago, Harvey had rescued Elias after I sent him to his room, sneaking him out for chocolate cake at their favorite bakery. That father has vanished.

In the end, Harvey barely notices Chloe is there.

Maybe it's all the drugs that help him sleep. What's worse is when he wakes up.

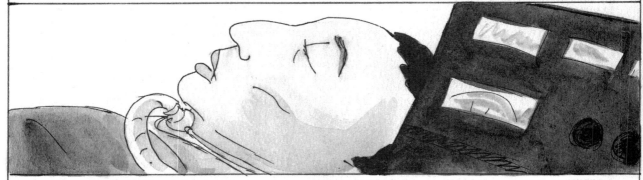

No matter how horrible all this is for me, it's a million times worse for Harvey. I'm torn apart, but he's being eaten up, bit by remorseless bit.

Another List

A few weeks after finding Harvey's first note about whether or not to get the trach, I find another despairing list.

What's going on? Why are you so stymied and depressed, indifferent to colleagues & wife, feeling inferior?

Eyes and wall of distance and disorientation?

Inability to concentrate & focus, distracted by detail & clutter & trivia in office & life; no priorities unless panic.

Colleagues snub last term, relief that out, difficulties at every faculty meeting; you're withdrawing. Not as eloquent as others. Nothing to say.

Breathless. Overdependence on Marissa.

Bad shape.
Seem hopelessly behind on book; outlived.
Do you really want to teach still? Is there any pleasure in it anymore?
Higher stakes now. Can you do it?
How to snap out of it.
Exercise
Task by task
Finish book
JUST DO IT!

I wish he could share this with me, that I could help him through it. All I can do is be with him, be with his pain and terror. I promise myself that I won't let him down, that I'll give his sons his values and interests as much as I can.

Besides his book, the only thing that interests Harvey now is Jewish ritual. Shabbat has always been central to our family, a time to be together.

But saying the blessings isn't a comfort anymore, only a sad reminder of what we no longer share.

At least, that's how I feel. Harvey shifts his focus from Friday nights to Saturdays when our congregation holds Shabbat services. We used to go a couple of times a month. Now Harvey goes most Saturdays.

GOOD SHABBOS.

Good Shabbos, Harvey.

He arranges to go with a friend who works with cancer patients. Alison scopes out where to plug in the ventilator, where to go for suctioning. She's patient and kind.

ALISON IS OUT OF TOWN. CAN YOU TAKE ME TO SHUL TODAY?

Of course.

I don't want to face all the people I know with their well-meaning sympathy. But if Harvey can do it, how can I refuse?

נפשי ישובב ינחנ‍י‍ ב‍מעגלי‍־‍צדק למען שמו

There's a lot of standing, then sitting, then standing again in Jewish ritual. Part of me is proud that Harvey refuses to give in to the disease, that he insists on standing. But mostly I resent the risk he's taking.

I love the familiar Shabbat prayers, the melodies that Jews have sung for millennia. They fill me with sadness.

We've been going to Netivot Shalom since the congregation first started with a handful of families looking to build a conservative tradition (in Berkeley, of all places!). Our family grew with the shul. Simon was in the first preschool class, Harvey wrote the bylaws, I chaired the committee that hired our first principal.

לום במרומיו הוא יעשה שלו

I hope Harvey gets something out of Shabbat, some connection to a greater meaning. I feel left with no meaning at all.

I'm losing so many facets of Harvey, I can't grasp them all, but here's another one. Of course I was Jewish before I met him and I'll be Jewish after he dies, but who I am as a Jew was strongly shaped by him.

What kind of Jew will I be without him? And what will Netivot Shalom mean to me without him there?

It's easier for me to avoid shul. I'm relieved that Alison can take Harvey the next Saturday.

For me, managing challah, candles, and wine on Friday night is enough.

Anyway, I have to focus on how Harvey can teach in the fall. He insists he can give a seminar. His role model is Stephen Hawking.

The computer speaks for me.

Nobody complains about his singsong digital voice.

Cathy, the neurologist at the ALS Clinic, meets with us to figure out what we need.

You'll need a power wheelchair in a few months, Harvey.

You'll be too weak to walk by then.

That's because he doesn't have ALS.

He must have MS or something else. No one with ALS has ever been stable that long. No one.

MAYBE I'LL STAY THE SAME. HAWKING HASN'T CHANGED IN YEARS.

Harvey's face hardens, but I appreciate Cathy's bluntness.

I CAN STILL USE A SPEECH COMPUTER LIKE HIM.

Yes, you can, but it's not medically necessary, so your insurance won't pay for it, like they pay for nurses. Like they will for the wheelchair.

Anyway, the university should cover that. It's accommodation, allowing you to teach, so that falls under the Americans with Disabilities Act.

Harvey actually seems cheerfully excited at the thought of teaching. He's happy to track down the person at the university health services to talk to about the computer.

So why do I feel defeated, drained?

With the help of nurses, I can lead a normal life. But I don't feel normal. I feel like a zombie, walking among the living.

I'm envious of everyone I see. I want a life like theirs.

I want to take the ordinary for granted.

It turns out, I can't even take nurses for granted. Bonnie gives us notice.

I love working here, but my fiance can't find a job. The Bay Area is too expensive to live on one salary. We're moving back to Texas next week.

I'll miss the professor.

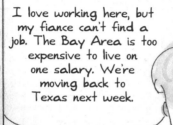

Jean comes to our rescue. She's only been working Saturday, but now she gives us her day off and switches with other nurses so we are covered for three days.

She's worked with ALS patients before, but never as early in the progression of the disease. Usually a nurse isn't needed until the end since the lungs are the last to go. Except in Harvey's case.

Jean dresses stylishly, not in "nurse clothes," as Simon calls them. She asks the boys about their homework. She even walks our pet turtle, Yertle.

There's something meditative about walking a turtle.

Yes, like watching grass grow.

Take a break. Have some tea.

I'm fine.

I don't want you to burn out.

And I rely on her to tell me the truth about Harvey.

I keep asking Harvey to let me tighten the trach collar, but he won't. It's so loose, I'm afraid the trach will fall out.

It already has.

WHAT?!

His neck is so weak, he walks stooped over and the trach fell out yesterday.

I didn't have time to get a new one, so I quickly rinsed it off and stuck it back in. He bled a bit, but he could breathe.

Would I be able to do that?

It's not easy and I've done it before. I'd hate for you to have to try.

Harvey must have been terrified!

But he still insists on keeping the collar loose.

Why does he make bad choices like that? Does part of him want to die?

No, he's afraid of dying. But denial can go a long way to cloud clear thinking. And he's deep in denial.

Of course he is! Cathy said it could take a year to come terms with the ALS diagnosis. Harvey's had four months.

But he's thinking clearly enough to admit that teaching might be too hard. He makes an appointment with the retirement benefits office to talk about early retirement instead. We face the usual stares.

The short trip exhausts Harvey and he collapses as soon as we get home.

MARISSA, WHAT DID SHE SAY?

The woman at the benefits office? You don't remember?

THE WALK WAS TOO LONG.

Harvey is so worn out by a hundred yards of walking, he hasn't focused on a word. We've put it off long enough — it's time to order the power wheelchair.

But first we meet with someone else at the university. This time about the speech computer, in case Harvey feels up to teaching.

What's wrong with him?

Don't worry — it's not contagious.

HELLO, HARVEY.

He's not deaf.

SPEECH COMPUTER

You can be involved at the end of the conversation. I need to talk to Harvey now.

She rattles off a long list of questions — what classes does he plan to teach, will he keep office hours, will he serve on departmental committees, what part of his job description can he still fill. Harvey answers politely. Not me.

Harvey chaired the art history department. He's served on endless committees, enough for three professors' lifetimes, especially when you consider all those difficult, senile, or incompetent professors who are actively discouraged from any administrative work.

Yet somehow, they still teach.

Well, how are you going to get to class?

But how will you get to campus?

I'M GETTING A POWER WHEELCHAIR. NOW HERE'S THE COMPUTER I NEED.

I'll drive him! Or he can take paratransit. Or a cab.

It's none of your business how he gets to class!

Have you budgeted for that?

SPEECH COMPUTER

If Harvey's teaching, there's no reason to worry about a budget!

NOW WHEN CAN HE GET THE COMPUTER?!

Weeks go by with no word about the computer. Harvey emails several times. I call Ms. Ice every day. Nothing. Finally, I call a friend who specializes in workplace discrimination. She gives me the legal terms I need to press a claim. The next day, Harvey gets an email that the computer has been approved.

Not soon enough.

SPEECH COMPUTER

Getting the power wheelchair is easy after fighting with the university. Easy for me, not for Harvey.

Can I try one out?

This one is cool! I could ride in your lap, Dad!

How much battery life does that thing have?

An hour. That's enough time to pick out a chair?

Guess it has to be.

I'm not as worried as the salesman, now that we have an adapter so we can plug the ventilator into the car the way you charge a cell phone. No more dragging around the heavy external battery, just in case.

I win!

No, I win!

I want a rematch!

I WANT SOMETHING SLEEKER.

I don't think they have a racing model.

From the prescription your doctor wrote, you need a tiltable seat to prevent bed sores, a neck rest for when you can't hold up your head, broad armrests so you can strap down your arms.

I GUESS THIS MODEL WILL DO.

Great. I'll contact the manufacturer to be sure they can mount the ventilator securely. Meanwhile you can think about colors. It'll take six to eight weeks to deliver.

Personally, I recommend the yellow be-cause you'll be on a crowded campus.

You'd be amazed how many people, especially cyclists, run into wheel-chairs. That's why it's called 'safety' yellow.

IT'S NOT SAFETY YELLOW. IT'S BILE YELLOW.

Pee yellow!

Can I drive your wheelchair when it comes? I'll be careful!

They're too little, but once I get my driver's license in two years, you can let me!

109

Not long after wheelchair shopping, after the boys are in bed . . .

What happened?

BEEP
BEEP
BEEP
BEEP
BEEP

I DON'T KNOW. . . THE PLUG CAME OUT AND WHEN I BENT DOWN TO PLUG IT BACK IN, I FELL.

I've just gotten Harvey upright when his legs buckle and he starts to fall again. He's lost forty pounds, he's rail thin, but still hard for me to pick up.

Harvey, are your legs getting weaker?

NO! I'M JUST DIZZY.

I'M PROBABLY TAKING TOO MANY SEDATIVES. I'LL EMAIL CATHY AND ASK HER IN THE MORNING.

I'll talk to Cathy, too. Are you okay now? Does your head hurt?

I'M FINE. I JUST NEED AN ATIVAN.

That'll just make you even more lightheaded.

The next morning, Harvey remembers nothing.

I WOULD REMEMBER IF I FELL.

What about the bump on back of your head?

I COULD HAVE GOTTEN THAT ANYWHERE. I DIDN'T FALL.

Harvey doesn't email Cathy, but I call her.

Is the ALS spreading to his legs or is it all the drugs he's taking? And what about his forgetting it even happened?

His legs are probably fine. We'd have to do another EMG to know for sure, but we usually do those once a year. He had one four months ago when he was diagnosed.

Drop the sleeping pill. The other drugs he's on will help him sleep anyway. If he continues to fall, we'll do an EMG, just so we can know what to expect.

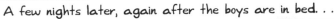

A few nights later, again after the boys are in bed. . .

BEEP BEEP
BEEP BEEP
BEEP BEEP

I race to get the ventilator and reconnect it.

What were you thinking? Why didn't you bring the ventilator with you or honk the horn to get me?

I THOUGHT I COULD DO IT.

Is it time for the EMG already? It's only April!

But Harvey refuses to go.

Please, Harvey!

NO!

Hours go by. The oxygen still hasn't come. Harvey's used up one tank and most of the second one. Jean leaves for her second shift with another patient.

I call Optal in a panic. The bored voice on the other ends says the oxygen will be delivered by seven p.m.

You can't get it here sooner?

We're short on drivers today.

It's after seven and still no oxygen. Harvey looks like he's made of wax. I call Cathy, terrified.

Call 911. The paramedics will hook him up to oxygen right away. They'll have to take him to the closest E.R., but we can have him transferred here later. The important thing is to get help. NOW.

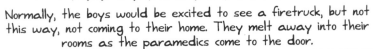

Normally, the boys would be excited to see a firetruck, but not this way, not coming to their home. They melt away into their rooms as the paramedics come to the door.

Simon, you're in charge.

I'll be at the hospital with Dad.

Instead of going to Monterey, Harvey spends spring break in the critical care unit. By the time a bed opens up in San Francisco, Harvey doesn't want to be moved, so Cathy can't run the test she wants.

If the pneumonia was caused by aspirating food, it's time for a feeding tube. And we need a neuropsych test to see what's going on with his thinking.

Cathy, you said his mind wouldn't be affected.

There's a percentage of ALS patients with cognitive issues.

But it's still spring break for the boys. I visit Harvey in the mornings and evenings. In between, I go out with the boys.

BING DING

BUZZZ

DONG

PING PING

ZZZ

EEEP

The arcade is noisy and chaotic — and peaceful for me.

Back at the hospital, the ventilator's alarm keeps going off.

I'm so sorry, Harvey. I can't make it stop. I'll call Optal for a new one.

BEEP BEEP!

We've gone through two ventilators already.

The next morning, there's a new, quiet ventilator. And a visit from Dr. Prentiss, the pulmonologist.

You should go into pulmonary rehab from here. We have other patients on ventilators there and they get excellent care without stressing their families.

But Harvey can take care of himself. And we have nurses helping.

You'll have to make this decision eventually. It's much easier to admit him straight from the hospital.

If you try once he's home, you might not get a place.

WE'LL THINK ABOUT IT.

Good! You really should!

But neither of us has any intention of considering medical warehousing. Instead, I spend five hours on the phone arranging Harvey's discharge.

CATHETERS, GLOVES, TUBES, ETC.

Now we have a new piece of equipment, an oxygen concentrator, a machine that transforms regular air into almost pure oxygen. That way we don't have to depend on Optal delivering supplies. Or so I think.

I bring Harvey home, thinner than ever. Asa and Simon seem afraid of him, but Elias still tells Harvey about his day. It's his after-school ritual. And he still comes to kiss him goodnight, undeterred by Harvey's lank mouth and drool.

And we're doing a cool science project.

Well, see ya.

Not that Harvey says anything back.

Harvey's been so closed off, I'm surprised when he suggests going out for our anniversary.

I WANT TO GO SOME PLACE NICE.

What a great idea!

The hostess isn't fazed when I ask for a table by an outlet. There are the usual stares, but no one asks what's wrong or what the ventilator is. I almost feel normal. Hopeful.

I THINK I'LL TEACH A SEMINAR ON GOTHIC SCULPTURE THIS FALL.

Should I propose a toast? To what? That we've made it this far?

CHAPTER FOUR IS ALMOST DONE. IN ANOTHER MONTH, MAYBE TWO, I CAN FINALLY FINISH THE BOOK. I'M GETTING CLOSE.

Mmmm.

I'm so used to careening from crises to crises, it's good to pause, to focus on each other.

THAT WAS NICE.

Happy anniversary.

OKAY...

Jean comes with us the following week for the EMG and neuropsych test. While Jean watches the EMG (so exciting!), I talk to Jessica, the doctor running the study on the cognitive effects of ALS. She has a long list of questions about Harvey.

What's troubling is that Harvey is consistently choosing badly. He doesn't seem to grasp the implications of what he does or doesn't do.

Will he still be able to teach?

That kind of knowledge shouldn't be impaired. It's executive functioning that's faulty.

Jessica says she'll call once she's gotten the test results. Now it's time for Cathy to talk to me about the EMG.

He would only let me do his left side, but there's clear weakness in his left arm and shoulder, the beginning of weakness in his leg.

You've ordered the wheelchair, right? Next, he'll have problems holding himself upright because of how impaired the muscles are around his lungs.

Already?

He'll still be able to type on the computer, won't he? Otherwise, he can't teach.

Oh sure. Those new computers are amazing. There's a device you can attach to his glasses so his blinking controls the mouse.

One last thing — call the Center for Independent Living and ask for a contractor to look at your house, figure out what you need to do to accommodate a wheelchair.

And that's a good thing? Harvey will be reduced to communicating through blinking? How is this happening so fast?

But Harvey insists he's as strong as ever.

YOU AND CATHY ALWAYS IMAGINE THE WORST.

LEAVE ME ALONE!

I manage to change nursing agencies, so Jean can be with us more days, and we have a new nurse, Cliff.

I appreciate that the nurses all call Harvey "Professor," a mark of respect that matters more than ever.

There now, Professor, that's better.

On Monday I get a call from Elias' teacher, the kind parents dread.

Last Friday, Elias and some other 5th graders were chasing a group of first graders. Things got pretty wild and three boys got hurt. We had a group of angry parents in here today asking for Elias to be suspended. We assured them that he's not a bully and that this won't happen again. We respect your family's privacy, of course, and didn't mention the situation at home. But we are concerned . . .

I'll be sure Elias apologizes.

The boys are okay?

I tell Harvey about the trouble at school.

TELL JEAN IT'S TIME FOR MY PILLS.

I'm alone in coping with Elias. With all of it.

I ask Elias about what happened on Friday and he starts crying.

I know how angry you are about Dad. I'm furious myself, but you can't hurt people.

I know!

I'm sorry, really sorry!

It's time for the kids in your class to know how sick Dad is. No more secrets.

Elias starts on his apology cards. He looks like a weight has been lifted.

I call the parents of the three boys — they're in Asa's class — and as much as I try to control myself, I can't help crying.

I'm so sorry, but I hope you understand the situation now.

Of course! How can we help?

We just have to get through this on our own.

But one of the mothers insists she can help. She tells the other families in Elias' and Asa's classes and they all take turns bringing us meals. The support is wonderful. And after all their worries, the boys don't feel stigmatized. They feel cared for. Harvey is the only one who resents the help. He sees it as another way I've failed.

I make one last call that night, to my brother.

I explain what happened to Steve.

This whole family is sick, not just Harvey. Can you and Debbie please take the boys on a vacation? Maybe to Mexico? Debbie's an expert on finding deals there and I don't care if they miss school.

Of course! It'll be fun!

Harvey didn't react to the news about Elias' school problem, but he's furious when I tell him the boys might go away with Steve and Debbie.

IF THEY'RE GOING TO MEXICO, WE'RE GOING, TOO.

They need a break from a sick dad and a stressed-out mom.

YOU'RE EXAGGERATING AS USUAL. IF WE'RE NOT GOING, THEY CAN'T GO.

They need this trip without us.

I have to be firm. I have to be.

THERE YOU ARE, BEING HIGH-HANDED AGAIN! JUST BECAUSE I'M SICK DOES NOT MEAN I CAN'T MAKE DECISIONS ABOUT THIS FAMILY ANYMORE. YOU DON'T ASK ME. YOU TELL ME.

He's right, but I don't feel I have a choice. I'm taking care of the boys. Harvey's taking care of himself.

That week Jessica calls to give me the results of the neuropsych test. When someone says they don't want to alarm you, they're about to do just that.

Harvey's very intelligent, so he can finesse his way through a lot of things. I want to reassure you that he can certainly teach.

"The problem is there's a lack of empathy. For example, he can't identify the difference between a sad or angry face. He's not intentionally cold or cruel. He simply can't grasp feelings."

"He's also lost executive functioning, the ability to understand cause and effect, the consequences of actions. That won't interfere with teaching, though he may need help organizing and grading the class."

"It means you have to make decisions for Harvey. He can no longer make them for himself. Think about what he would have wanted when he was well and use that as your guide."

Jessica agrees not to tell Harvey any of this. Instead she emails him that the results are normal.

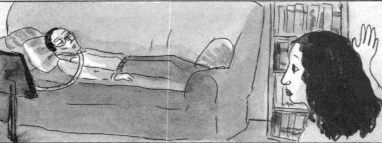

I know what she's saying. I'll have to decide when Harvey goes off the ventilator. He no longer can.

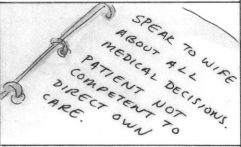

SPEAK TO WIFE ABOUT ALL MEDICAL DECISIONS. PATIENT NOT COMPETENT TO DIRECT OWN CARE.

And an ugly new page is added to the nurses' binder.

Debbie works her usual magic and finds a good last-minute airfare to Puerta Vallarta. She even arranges for a villa, complete with a cook.
Perfect timing since it's now mid-May, just in time for Simon's 14th birthday.

I want a ride!

Let's race!

I'm sorry, but you need a notarized statement from both parents giving permission for the children to leave the country.

But I called the airline and they said a signed statement was fine. I specifically asked if it had to be notarized.

The agent explains that for Mexico, the permission has to be notarized. She asks how quickly Harvey can come to the airport, since they have a notary there. Or he can go to a notary near our home and fax the permission.

I hate myself for doing it, it seems like such a betrayal, but I don't know how else to get the boys on their flight.

I call Jean and explain what needs to be done.

What if I call the nurse who's with my husband right now and have her fax you the results of a recent neuropsych test that gives me decision-making power over my husband?

I win!

Asa, you're too heavy!

I guess that would work.

A few nerve-wracking minutes later, the fax sputters through.

I sign my own statement with the airport notary, then kiss the boys goodbye.

Bye, Mom!

Bye!

Bye!

They're blissfully unaware of how close they came to missing their trip.

As soon as I get home from the airport, I know something's wrong.

Harvey saw the paper!

I didn't know how to use the fax machine, so I had to ask him to show me.

Of course he wanted to see what I was sending.

What can I possibly say? I have to think of something.

Um. . . you saw the paper about the neuropsych test?

YES! I'M EMAILING CATHY RIGHT NOW FOR AN EXPLANATION!

WHAT A PACK OF LIES!

I'M PERFECTLY COMPETENT!

Of course you're competent.

SO IS THIS JUST ANOTHER EXAMPLE OF YOU TAKING CONTROL OF MY LIFE?

I'm stunned by his bitterness, like a punch in the gut.

No! It's just a way of justifying the expense of nurses to the insurance company. Since you can suction yourself, they're saying you don't need nurses.

THEY'RE RIGHT. I DON'T!

Is he buying this? He seems a little softer.

LET'S SEE WHAT CATHY HAS TO SAY. AND TELL JEAN I'M THIRSTY.

I'm dismissed.

I page Cathy and as usual, she calls right back.

Don't worry, I'll say the same thing you did. And I'll tell him I've already let the university know there's no medical reason he can't teach.

That'll make him feel better.

I imagine the boys swimming in the warm Mexican sun as I swim in the cool dark mornings. I hope they're getting the vacation they need and not thinking about any of this.

Asa calls every night from Puerta Vallarta.

I want to see you, Mom!

Aren't you having fun?

Yesssss.

But I miss you!

Debbie tries to reassure me.

He's fine during the day. He only remembers to miss you at night. He has a lot of nightmares.

The bracelet isn't working?

We're getting a new one tomorrow. Don't worry — he's having fun, really.

Maybe I need a bracelet to keep my own nightmares away.

The weekend the boys are gone happens to be time for the regular ALS support group meeting. We haven't been since February, when Harvey got the trach, so now we're dismayed to learn that Millie, Trisha, and Shelly, all of whom had Bulbar ALS like Harvey, have died.

Carl, who showed off his feeding tube in December, is now confined to a wheelchair.

David, the other man with Bulbar ALS, can still walk, but now has a feeding tube.

I brought the video of me hang gliding. I still get around.

If people are shocked by how much Harvey has deteriorated, no one says so. It's the kind of group where devastating declines are the norm, and you never know from month to month who will die.

In the car on the way home, the ventilator alarm goes off.

What's the matter? What does the ventilator say?

IT SAYS BAT LOW.

BEEP BEEP

How can the battery be low? The LTV gets power through the charger plugged into the car.

IT'S NOTHING. THE ALARM IS ALWAYS GOING OFF.

BEEP BEEP BEEP

I take the next exit and pull into the first gas station I see.

BEEP BEEP BEEP

LET'S JUST GO HOME.

It's the charger! It's not working. All this time, the LTV has been using the internal battery and now there's nothing left! What are we going to do?

BEEP BEEP BEEP BEEP

Without power? I plug the ventilator into the gas station wall and call Optal.

But the home health company can't say when they'll be able to get us a new charger — big surprise. There's only one thing to do.

Here, take my jacket.

You'll have to stay here while I go home to get the external battery.

OKAY. JUST HURRY BACK.

123

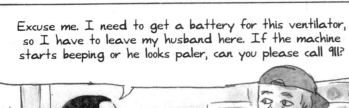
Excuse me. I need to get a battery for this ventilator, so I have to leave my husband here. If the machine starts beeping or he looks paler, can you please call 911?

Ok.

The attendant is so unfazed, I wonder what other odd requests he gets.

How ludicrous, plugging Harvey into a gas station wall. If it weren't so awful, it'd be funny.

I race home, then back to the gas station, and am hooking up the battery to the ventilator when Celia, from Optal, drives up. I'm a frazzled mess. She's elegant and calm.

The charger's defective. I'm sorry, but we don't have any in stock. We'll need to order a new one.

Um, thanks.

So why did you come?

This is what life is really about. Not ventilators or equipment failures or angry denial. If I have to go back to the land of ALS, at least I have our sons to remind me that our home is still full of life.

One of the moms in Simon's carpool suggests I talk to a therapist she knows. Why bother?

She's more than a therapist — she's someone who's gone through the same thing. Her husband died from ALS. And like Harvey, his symptoms began during a sabbatical year in Europe.

She just moved to Berkeley. How can you *not* see her?

I guess I can try one session.

Lauren, the therapist, clearly understands the burden I'm carrying and the loneliness of the journey, but she also sees Harvey's point of view.

Now he wants to get his license renewed and drive again. He can't — that's not safe.

That's his choice to make. He's your husband, not your child.

But he's acting like a two-year-old.

I don't dismiss her advice. I turn it over in my mind, waiting for the heft of it to feel right.

You're insisting that Harvey stay in a relationship with you, stay in your marriage. But he's already left.

There's no way to reach him? It's too late?

Lauren agrees to meet with Harvey by himself and then the two of us as a couple.

I feel an ember of hope that, with her help, Harvey and I might finally come together in our struggle with the disease, instead of each fighting it in our separate ways.

But how do I give Harvey more independence while planning for the opposite?

Martin, the contractor who specializes in making homes handicap-accessible, comes to assess our house.

Here's an easy change you can make — put a bar in the bathroom so Harvey can pull himself up from the toilet.

That will work as long as his arms are strong, but they're already getting weaker.

You can put a lift here, the kind where you strap Harvey in, then transfer him to and from the wheelchair on either end.

Don't you need to hold your body upright for that?

Yes.

The neurologist said those muscles will be the next to go.

It quickly becomes clear that Martin is used to people who know their limits, not ones like Harvey, where the limits constantly change.

Then you have to make a choice . . .

Once you decide which part of the house you want to be in, we can work on that section.

I WANT TO BE IN BOTH!

Harvey. . .

I'LL THINK ABOUT IT. GOOD BYE!

I know it's a brutal choice, but we can't afford to modify the whole house. I don't want to end up like Lauren, so much in debt from the huge expenses of ALS that she almost lost her home.

127

We didn't go to Mexico or Monterey, but I've booked flights for Dallas as soon as school gets out. Harvey wants to see his family and Cathy thinks we can manage. She arranges for a second external battery in case of flight delays and tells me to order oxygen directly from the airline.

I spend hours on the phone again. Besides the oxygen, I have to clear the use of the ventilator (an electronic device we can't turn off for takeoff and landing). I use miles for Harvey and me to fly in business class since we can't fit all his equipment in coach. What I really want to order is a wheelchair. I can't imagine how Harvey will make it through security, all the way to the gate, without one.

Harvey, of course, sees no need for any of this, and he's adamant that he's not using a wheelchair.

The week before the trip, we meet with Lauren. I hope she'll convince Harvey about the wheelchair.

What are you afraid will happen if Harvey walks?

That he'll fall.

Even if he doesn't hurt himself, that's a scary thing for the boys to see.

WHAT'S THE BIG DEAL ABOUT FALLING?

It's really Harvey's choice to make. You can't control the risks.

At the end of the session, Lauren gives us homework. Harvey is to consider how his actions affect others (except he can't). Mine is to allow Harvey to make his own mistakes (except I can't).

Talking with Lauren hasn't helped. Harvey's as cold and angry as ever. Maybe it's my fault for not giving in. I've been fighting to do what's best for the boys, but is that what's best for Harvey? I don't know anymore.

I'm sorry I argued with you about the wheelchair. It's fine if you don't want one.

Harvey, did you hear what I said? I'm sorry I've been so stubborn. I'll support whatever you want to do.

Harvey?

I HEARD YOU.

TELL JEAN TO BRING ME MY PILLS.

His words cut into me. There's no hope for a last-minute epiphany. The man I love is gone, buried so deeply by the disease, I'll never see him again.

129

After all the fighting, as soon as we get to the airport, Harvey says he's too tired to walk. I leave him with the boys while I go park the car.

130

We don't find a wheelchair, but we get a ride on an electric cart instead.

I've always wanted to ride on one of these!

This is as good as an amusement park!

Airport security is heightened and I'm worried the ventilator will look suspicious. I've brought a letter from Cathy, explaining why we have so many machines and batteries, but no one asks for it. They wave Harvey right through.

What's the matter with him?

ALS, Lou Gehrig's disease.

How did he get it?

Don't worry, it's rare. And not contagious.

Harvey collapses on the plane while Simon and I struggle with all the equipment.

Despite my many calls, the airline isn't prepared for us.

Folks, this is your captain. Sorry for the delay, but we needed to clear some special cargo. That's been taken care of and we're ready to push back from the gate now.

WHY ARE WE LATE?

You're the special cargo — or your ventilator is.

The flight is easy after all the stress leading up to it. There's a wheelchair waiting for us when we get off, and Harvey doesn't say a word, just sinks weakly into it. It's scary to see him like this, quiet and defeated.

Can we get BBQ?

We can't be in Dallas without BBQ!

Do I like BBQ?

Everyone gathers at Harvey's sister, Helen's, house for dinner. No one comments on what we're facing. They take in Harvey's gauntness, how much he's aged in the past seven months, how slurred his speech is, and carry on a conversation that's unfailingly polite and superficial. Exactly what Harvey wants.

My wish is that Harvey will be with us when Asa celebrates his own birthday in October.

I know it's early, ten days before your birthday, but since you're here, we should celebrate.

JUST LIKE MOTHER ALWAYS USED TO MAKE. I DIDN'T KNOW YOU HAD THE RECIPE ALL THESE YEARS.

Don't forget to make a wish!

I'll blow out the candles for you, Dad!

Tell me a story about Dad.

You're filming?

Simon, how have you been? How's school?

Ok.

The next day, we go to Sid's to see more relatives and old friends.

Harvey was fine yesterday. He loved the cake. But today, he's so tired, he can barely speak.

Something's wrong.

It's so nice to see you, Harvey!

So special!

Are you sure?

Maybe it's the excitement of seeing everyone?

Before we left Berkeley, Cathy gave me the phone number of an ALS doctor in Dallas. I describe Harvey's symptoms to him and he tells me to bring him to the E.R. He suspects pneumonia.

The boys go out for ice cream with Helen while Sid drives us to the hospital.

Yes, it's pneumonia.

Tell the boys we'll be back soon — and BBQ for dinner.

All the way to Dallas, and Harvey's back in the hospital.

In the hotel that night, I agonize over what to do. Our flight home is in two days.

Let's get more pillows from room service!

Hey, *Back to the Future* is on!

Should we stay or go? Harvey decides for me. And for once I don't argue. Because he's thinking of the boys.

The boys make early Father's Day cards and give them to Sid to pass on to Harvey.

TAKE THE BOYS HOME. THEY'LL GO CRAZY STUCK IN A HOTEL. YOU CAN COME BACK ONCE I'M READY TO LEAVE.

WELL, I'M READY NOW, BUT YOU KNOW WHAT I MEAN.

JUST GO.

He's stronger on the IV antibiotics, but the doctor says he needs to stay at least a week.

Dear Dad,
I love when you play with me.
I love when you make steak for me.
I love when you take me to the park. LOVE, ASA

Maybe I'm the one in denial now. It doesn't occur to me that Harvey might die. I trust the doctors caring for him. Dr. Vadim is a pulmonologist specializing in ALS, one of only two in the country.

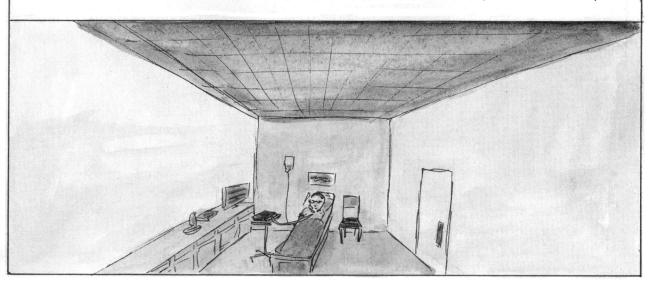

Still, it's hard to leave. Getting on a plane feels like a bad omen, like we'll never travel together as a family again.

Mr. Stahl? We have your oxygen for you.

NO! You have the wrong Mr. Stahl!

I told the gate agent my husband isn't on this flight. He's in the hospital.

It's a stupid mistake, but I feel a sharp sense of panic. I've been clinging to my kids as if they're a rope that can pull me safely to shore, to a normal life.

I can't bear to be reminded that I can't take their well-being for granted.

I can't take anything for granted.

Without the whoosh of the ventilator, I can sleep in our bed again instead of the living room sofa.

If I could sleep . . .

Things should be easier without having to care for Harvey. I can spend more time on my new project about a boy's life, inventions, and experiments — and dealing with his parents' divorce. I can't face writing about a father's death, but I can have my character figure out how to handle his new, fragmented family.

I talk to Dr. Vadim each day. He says Harvey's recovering from the pneumonia, but there are other issues we need to face.

Monday

Your husband has an accelerated course of the disease and his behavior is making the decline even quicker. If he doesn't make some serious changes, he'll have a drastic lessening of the quality of his life in the next few months.

Tuesday

He should have a feeding tube put in while he's here. Two cases of pneumonia in less than two months suggests he's aspirating his food. I've talked to his neurologist in San Francisco and she agrees with me.

Wednesday

As you can probably guess, Harvey insists he doesn't need a feeding tube. But if he keeps denying the obvious, things will soon deteriorate to the point where you can't care for him in your home.

Thursday

You need to convince him about the tube. That will buy him some time. He has to see how necessary it is.

Friday

Have you convinced him?

But I can't convince Harvey. He says he knows how to swallow and that Dr. Vadim has his own "agenda." What would that be, I ask, besides helping his patient?

I don't know what else to do, so I call hospice. Only it turns out that Harvey doesn't qualify since he's on a ventilator. I ask the case manager what to do. She agrees to approve another nursing shift — if we can find the nurses.

I'VE DECIDED TO GET THE FEEDING TUBE SO YOU'LL STOP NAGGING ME. DR. VADIM SAYS HE'LL RELEASE ME THE NEXT DAY. SO ARRANGE FOR A FLIGHT HOME WEDNESDAY.

You'll come home on your birthday? That's great!

It's a huge relief! Harvey will get better, at least for a little while.

Plus, the boys won't miss their dad's birthday, after missing Father's Day.

We need to pick out a present for Dad.

I want to get him a book about medieval manuscripts.

Me, too!

And we can make him a Welcome Home banner.

A seismic shift has jolted me onto new terrain. Now I'm more worried about how our sons deal with Harvey's illness than with caring for Harvey. The tug of war is over. I let go of the rope tethering me to Harvey, the one that makes me pull him against his will into our family. The boys have won, but it isn't Harvey who has lost. It's me.

Since I don't know how to deal with a feeding tube, Cathy suggests that Jean fly out to accompany Harvey home. The insurance pays for her time. I take care of her ticket.

Of course, I'll go. I've never been to Dallas.

I'll show you how to use the tube, keep it sanitary, once we're back.

The boys work on the banner in a frenzy to have the house perfect for their dad.

I follow up with the speech computer company and convince them to send us a loaner since Harvey is still on the wait list and impatient to learn the system. I call about the wheelchair which will arrive the following week. I even schedule a new DMV appointment for Harvey since he missed the last one.

Waiting at the arrivals area of the airport is agonizing. I haven't allowed myself to think about the possibility of him dying in Dallas, but it's been lurking in a deep corner of my mind, far down where I don't dare go.

And finally there he is, bone thin, but alive.

You look good.

AND YOU LOOK AS BEAUTIFUL AS EVER.

And there he is, for one magical moment, the man I've loved for so many years and missed so profoundly these past seven months.

And just as quickly, he's gone.

That was a hard trip — excruciating!

COME ON, LET'S GO!

It's not easy traveling with all this stuff. The feeding tube wasn't a problem since he refuses to use it.

I CAN SWALLOW FINE!

I don't even care about the tube. I'm just glad to have Harvey home.

Harvey opens himself up to the boys, there for them the way he was for me, that one brief glimpse at the airport.

WELCOME HOME, DAD!!!

Happy Birthday, Dad!

Happy Birthday!

And welcome home!

Harvey really looks at each of his sons, reads their cards, leafs through the book appreciatively. He's truly with them, giving them something they'll always have — his love.

You're a great father!

You taught me the finer things in life, such as wine, art, and religion. You continue to ensure that I'm well-rounded and balanced. You teach appreciation of character and depth. You provide a solid grounding for me and help me connect with family. You're always doing fun things with me from steam trains to the Exploratorium to Yosemite, movies, London and Cambridge, rockets, and hockey games.

Love, Simon

I should have written something, too, but I didn't. I couldn't face a blank page with all the feelings I have for Harvey. I don't dare think about all he means to me. Because that means realizing all I'm losing.

He looks like he's staring at death while he clings to his sons' lives.

Later, looking over the photos Jean took, I'm struck by the hollow ache in Harvey's eyes.

The next day, Harvey still won't use the feeding tube, but he eats well and seems to have more energy.

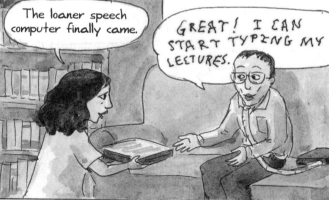

The loaner speech computer finally came.

GREAT! I CAN START TYPING MY LECTURES.

Maybe Dr. Vadim is wrong and things won't be so bad.

But the next day, Harvey is so weak, he asks for help getting dressed, something he's never done before.

You're losing so much weight. We've got to get more calories into you. Why not try the feeding tube?

I GOT THE TUBE SO THEY'D LET ME OUT OF THE HOSPITAL. I DON'T NEED IT.

ANYWAY, IT'S NOT EATING THAT'S THE PROBLEM. IT'S BREATHING.

All the tears I've been holding in for so long pour out in ragged sobs.
I don't care if Harvey sees me crying. I can't be strong anymore. I'm terrified.

145

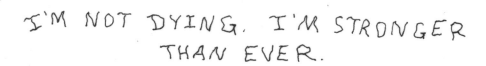

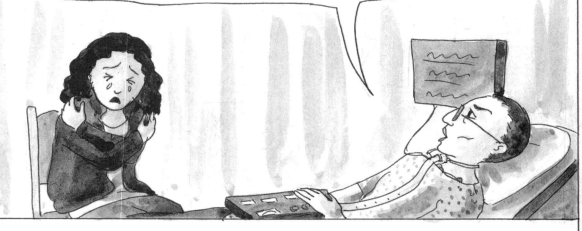

I can't bear the thought of his death. I need more time, just a little more time. I want to throw my arms around him, to fold myself up against his chest, to beg him not to leave me. But his eyes are hard and cold. He won't even look at me.

I'm still crying an hour later when the pulmonologist walks in. It's the same doctor who tried to talk us into pulmonary rehab.

Is it true you think Harvey should go home?

Well, it's six of one, half a dozen of another. If he stays, he could be exposed to some of the nasty bugs common in a hospital.

He can just as easily take antibiotics at home. Here's the prescription.

But shouldn't he get stronger IV antibiotics? Doesn't he need to be hydrated? Plus, it's hard for him to swallow pills.

You can crush the pills and put them in the feeding tube. It's easy.

IT'S FRIDAY. I WANT TO BE HOME FOR SHABBAT.

I know this is hard for you.

I can see that the doctor is thinking I should have put Harvey in pulmonary rehab when we had the chance and we're paying for our bad decision. If that's the choice, I'll take Harvey home and the doctor can go to hell.

I'll tell the nurse to get your paperwork so you can sign it and go home.

THANK YOU!

Thanks for nothing!

I WANT TO BE HOME FOR SHABBAT.

I haven't had time to buy challah and chicken for our traditional Friday night meal. What kind of Shabbat will it be anyway?

By now it's 6 p.m. Harvey has been in the same cubicle for seven hours. We've been waiting for the paperwork for almost an hour and Harvey's had enough. He tears off the monitoring leads, shoves on his pants and sandals, picks up the ventilator, and walks out.

I hurry after him, shocked that he has so much strength when before he could barely stand.

Fueled by will alone, he strides out of the emergency room, making it all the way to the bench outside before he sits down to catch his breath.

I do what he says. And I'm proud of him.

Without eating anything myself — when had I last eaten? — I rush to feed Harvey and the boys, then hurry to the pharmacy, furious now at Harvey for choosing badly. At myself for helping him.

Harvey finally eats. Slowly. Deliberately. While I wolf down some yoghurt.

THAT'S ALL YOU'RE HAVING? IT'S SHABBAT.

Yes, it's Shabbat, but all I can manage is opening a container and shoveling the contents into my mouth.

I wish desperately that someone would take care of me, make my meals, wash my clothes, buy my challah.

HACKKK HAKKK

I wish that person was my husband.

Harvey got the antibiotics down, but he can't swallow the Ativan, the anti-anxiety drug he takes. He keeps pushing the pill with his finger as far back in his mouth as he can, then pouring water on his tongue. But he can't get the thin, small disc down his throat. His tongue sits heavy and still in his mouth, another muscle he no longer controls.

Do you want me to crush the pill and put it in the feeding tube?

NO!

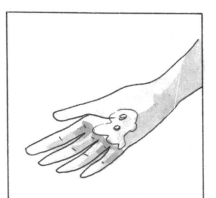

He simply can't swallow. Water dribbles out of his mouth, spills on his shirt. Finally, he gives up.

The pace of the disease still surprises me. We plunge down its steep slope, flailing desperately to stay upright, until we skid to a halt. Before we have time to assess the new landscape, the ground shifts again, pulling us down with it. There is no status quo to get used to, only the dizzying wrenching of our feet out from under us, the powerful, inexorable avalanche of the disease's progression.

When my grandfather died, my sister and I spent the night at his side, crooning the old show tunes he loved so much, stroking him so he knew he wasn't alone on his journey.

When I take you out tonight with me . . .

Honey, here's the way it's gonna be . . .

As he took his last rattling breath, I felt an enormous release. Sad as I was for him to go, his death was his final gift to me. I had the sense of being a midwife to him, helping him find his way to die. Peacefully. There are good deaths.

Harvey's journey isn't like that at all. He's being ripped from his life before he's ready to leave it. Neither of us has the luxury of time for the necessary mental, emotional, and spiritual preparation.

Good night. I love you.

We're engulfed, swept up, losing ourselves in the process, beating our fists and roaring NOOOOO! The whole way.

Dying well means accepting death, just as an easy birth means yielding to the overwhelming pain, moving through it, not resisting. Neither of us knows how to do that. Neither of us has had the time to move beyond shock and despair to acceptance.

Early the next morning a
noise jars me awake.

Harvey's fallen. He's holding a suction catheter and the ventilator is disconnected, like he was trying to suction himself. His eyes are open, but he doesn't see me.

I reconnect the ventilator and call 911.

Ten molasses minutes later, the paramedics arrive.

Haven't we been here before?

He's dying, he's dying, he's dying . . .

There's no rise to his chest. No beating to his heart. He's still as stone.

I'm sorry.

Is there someone we can call for you?

Here is the moment I've dreaded. Harvey's dead and I'm unmoored from reality. Would gravity still hold my feet to the ground? Would the sun still rise and set? Would my own heart keep beating without his to accompany it? I stare at Harvey's face, empty of that tremendous will that allowed him to pick up the ventilator and walk out of the emergency room.

I steady my breathing, trying to think, but I've lost all sense of myself. Part of me has been ripped out of my chest and vanished, along with Harvey.

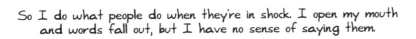
So I do what people do when they're in shock. I open my mouth and words fall out, but I have no sense of saying them.

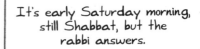
It's early Saturday morning, still Shabbat, but the rabbi answers.

Call the rabbi. I have to call the rabbi!

I don't want to do anything against Jewish law.

Stu? Harvey's dead.

I'll be right there and take care of everything. I'll call the mortuary and the chevra kadisha.

Can you call your family?

Shelah, who rarely travels, is away on business in Korea. Steven and Debbie are in DC, but within an hour, the rabbi, my parents, and my youngest brother, Brion, are all here. Somehow the boys have slept through it all. It's not yet seven am.

It's time you woke up the children and tell them what's happened.

I can't think of how best to deliver such awful news. I'm a creature of instinct, fumbling my way through the dark days ahead.

I shake Simon awake and instead of him growling at me to let him sleep, he waits for me to say the words he expects.

Death has already stiffened Harvey's face. His skin is waxy pale, but I ask the boys if they want to see their father before the mortuary comes for his body.

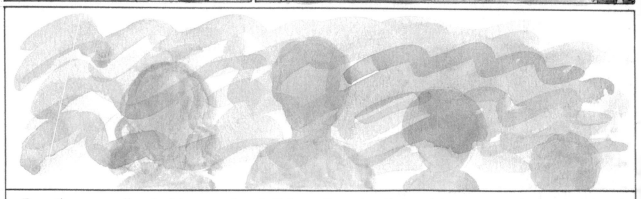

I can't say exactly what happened next. I know I cried until Asa told me to stop it. I know Simon bleached his hair that night, transforming his brunette curls to blond. I wish I could make such a clear statement of the transformation our lives have undergone, and I silently congratulate him on the aptness of his symbolic choice. He's still a teenager, not the man of the family. That's my job now.

As promised, the rabbi takes care of everything. The chevra kadisha, members of our congregation, will ritually wash and wrap the body, place it in a simple wooden coffin. All we have to do is choose a plot in the Jewish section of the cemetery.

In Judaism, the funeral happens as quickly as possible. We wait a day, so family has time to come — Harvey's Dallas family, Shelah from Korea, Steven and Debbie from DC. The body isn't left alone from death to burial, and the chevra kadisha, along with family members, have taken the other shifts, leaving us with the last one, the final hour before the service.

That last hour, alone with Harvey and our memories, is the beginning of our healing. I wish I had said the blessings for Harvey that Friday night, that I had given him that one last Shabbat he so desperately wanted. I wish I hadn't been so angry at him for choosing to come home and die. I wish it could have ended differently, with me telling him how much I loved him and him telling me the same.

The service goes by in a blur. But there's a grim finality to shoveling three scoops of earth, hearing them thud on the coffin. As Asa struggles with the shovel, I'm frozen. Finally, his cousin Liisa, the one with the magical bracelets, helps him, and I can breathe again in giant silent sobs.

My older sister chooses this moment to offer her condolences.

Doesn't Daniel look handsome in his dress uniform?

Her son Daniel wears his Marine dress parade uniform. Maybe he's handsome.
But I'm watching my child bury his father.

And then it's over . . . until next year when we'll unveil the headstone.

The Book

Harvey doesn't leave letters for the boys to open on their birthdays. Instead, he leaves a fourth child, the book he hasn't finished.

I go through his notes, stacks of them written in his cramped handwriting, search his emails, hoping to find a student or colleague to finish it for him.

But there's nobody. Only me.

I don't know medieval French. I detest footnotes and any writing that includes words like "hermeneutics." But I'm a writer. I tell myself I can do this.

Writing is a way for me to find myself again and to reclaim Harvey, who he was before he got sick. Reading his words is like having a conversation with him again, hearing how he thinks, his passion for art and history. The last chapter of the book is especially moving. Harvey argues that Louis IX chose specific Old Testament stories to focus on as a way to educate his sons. Psalters were used as teaching tools for the well-born and Louis wanted his sons to be good kings, moral kings.

He ends the psalter on a strange note. The ancient Israelites have begged God for a king. God discourages them, telling them to rule themselves. But they want a powerful king like other nations have. So God sets Saul as a king over them. Only it turns out that Saul is a bad king, making rash mistakes.

The lesson Louis is giving his sons is that kingship is a responsibility. During this time when kings ruled by divine right, Louis wanted his sons to be humble, not arrogant, to choose to be good kings who took care of their subjects.

This is what Harvey worked so hard on instead of writing letters to his own sons. It's part of his legacy to them. He, like Saint Louis, wanted his sons to be good kings.

Picturing Kingship

History and Painting in the Psalter of Saint Louis

Harvey Stahl

I turn to medieval scholars all over the world, people who knew and loved Harvey. And with their help, I even manage to write footnotes. It takes four years, but I finish the last chapters based on talks Harvey had given along with his notes and outlines. I find a publisher, order photographs from museums all over the world, request permissions in three different languages.

It's a great collaborative effort. I wish Harvey could see it. I wish he could have known I would do this for him.

The Boys

Like me, Simon finds his way through stories. He spends that summer in his room, becoming a cartoonist. The words and pictures are something to hold onto as he gropes his way to defining himself as a man without his father to guide him.

For Elias, the veil of illusion we all maintain that bad things don't happen arbitrarily has been torn away. He stockpiles water under his bed, sleeps with a knife in easy reach.

I thought I would always be happy.

Just because one horrible thing happened, doesn't mean the rest of your life will be bad.

I hope someday he — and I — can believe that.

At the mention of Harvey, Asa runs away with his hands over his ears. He blames me for letting his father die — and not digging him up and bringing him back once he's buried.

First Things

Almost a year exactly from when Harvey had the tracheotomy, 8 months after his death, I'm invited to a school in Casablanca as a visiting author.

While I'm gone, the boys stay with my brothers, my sister, my parents, a patchwork of childcare that works despite all the seams.

I'm proving that I can travel without Harvey. I hope to impress myself with how strong I can be as a woman in an Arab country, but something else happens.

The school puts me up with a Moroccan family who welcome me warmly into their home.

They take me to see the sights, invite me to the hamman, to have henna on my hands.

A baby girl was born to the father's brother, and like the bris in Judaism, there's a Muslim ritual on the 8th day after birth — for a girl, a naming ceremony.

This is the author, Marissa Moss.

She's staying with us.

I hope you'll come to the naming.

Congratulations on your beautiful daughter!

The whole family gathers at the grandfather's home. I'm touched to be included.

In one song, the new mother is surrounded by other women who dance with her, celebrating her return to the community. I'm swept up in the beauty of the ritual, honored to be part of it all.

Come dance with us.

In my old life, before Harvey was sick, I would have felt too self-conscious to stand up. I would have shaken my head, smiling, and continued in my role as spectator. But I felt Harvey urging me on.

He never let something as silly as embarrassment or vanity get in the way of a new experience. When we were first married, we'd taken a trip to Amsterdam and stumbled on an exhibit of art from Dutch children's books. This was before I got published.

I love this woman's work.

Look, she lives in Amsterdam. Why don't you call her and meet her? She might have some advice.

My Dutch isn't good enough. She'll think I'm a nut.

The worst she can say is no. But what if she says yes?

To my surprise, the woman invited me to coffee the next day. She was generous with information and I learned a lot.

I think about that now, how the risk was tiny in contrast to the gain.

Harvey isn't there to push me forward into the group of dancers, yet he is somehow. As I stand up and start twirling, the only Western woman among them — and a Jew at that — I don't feel self-conscious at all. I lose myself in the music, the joy, the moment.

And I feel that I, too, like the new mother, am welcomed back to the world of the living.

Author's Note

The years after Harvey's death weren't easy, but I did one thing right — I made sure every winter break we took a Stahl Family vacation. These trips were different from the kind of travel we'd done with Harvey, to historical and artistic sites. Instead, we combined nature, hiking, art, and culture.

We climbed volcanoes in Indonesia, scaled Mt. Kilimanjaro, hiked the Inca trail to Machu Picchu. Most of all, we bonded as a family, coming out stronger from the loss of Harvey, rather than fracturing apart.

The boys are all young men now, and we're all different people from who we were before Harvey's death. Simon studied Computer Science and Animation at Northwestern and now designs children's books. Elias was a history major at the University of Toronto, then joined the Israeli army, in a special forces unit, something I doubt he would have done had his father lived. He's now in graduate school at the School for Advanced International Studies in DC, a much safer place to be. Asa is a Physics major at Johns Hopkins. I'm deeply proud of how they've each grown into capable, sensitive, interesting young men, all with strong values and senses of themselves.

For years, I couldn't imagine or plan for a future, nothing more than a few months out, because something bad could happen at any moment. That dread took a long time to dissipate and is still there, just not as pervasive. I didn't expect to remarry, wasn't looking for a new partner, but one found me, a wonderful man who was willing to take on a complicated family.

There's a part of Harvey I keep alive in me. I take the risks he would have wanted me to — and not just dancing in Morocco. A few years ago, I started a children's publishing company, Creston Books. We've gotten a lot of starred reviews, made some high-profile lists, even won some awards. I couldn't have done any of it without Harvey.

He'll always be with me in the ways that matter most.

Acknowledgments

This book was many, many years in the making and I relied on a community of writers and readers to help me along the way. I owe thanks to these people for their support, encouragement, and criticism (all essential to making the strongest book possible): Charlie Jane Anders, Bill Boerman-Cornell, Adrienne Boutang, Kathleen Caldwell, Gennifer Choldenko, Diane Fraser, Lauren Fishbein, Sari Friedman, Lisa Kaborycha, Mollie Katzen, Golda Laurens, Joan Lester, Ian Lendler, Wendy Lichtman, Elizabeth Partridge, Emily Polsby, Luisa Smith, Eleanor Vincent, Ellery Washington, and Cathleen Young. If I left anyone out, it's only because the book took me so long to write and it's hard to keep track of everyone I showed it to.

I owe the title to Joanne Rocklin — thank you!

This book wasn't easy to sell. Many agents and editors felt it was too dark or sad. I'm deeply grateful to my agent, Liza Fleissig, of the Liza Royce Agency, for her unwavering support for this story. It found the perfect home in Conari, with insightful editor Christine LeBlond, creative director Kathryn Sky-Peck, Bonni Hamilton, Debra Woodward, and nameless others I haven't yet met but who believed in the project and helped make this book. Thank you all for being part of my village!

When it came to the art, I relied on my eldest son, Simon, who worked as art director for the book. He designed a font based on my handwriting, set all the lettering, and used digital magic to clean up my hand-drawn work. I'm fortunate to have him help in a very concrete way.

I also want to thank Harvey's close friends who were so kind and supportive as we struggled to deal with the aftermath of his death. Harvey was fortunate to have many long, deep friendships. Rene Eksl, Peter Gruen, Alan Haufrect, and Stacy Roback were like brothers to him. Marie-Helene Berard, Anne Elliott, Marie-Jose LeBreton, Sarna Sunshine, and Karen Wold were his sisters. All of them are family to us still.

Most of all, I want to thank all three of my sons, Simon, Elias, and Asa, who read this book just last year and gave me permission to publish it.

To Our Readers

Conari Press, an imprint of Red Wheel/Weiser, publishes books on topics ranging from spirituality, personal growth, and relationships to women's issues, parenting, and social issues. Our mission is to publish quality books that will make a difference in people's lives—how we feel about ourselves and how we relate to one another. We value integrity, compassion, and receptivity, both in the books we publish and in the way we do business.

Our readers are our most important resource, and we appreciate your input, suggestions, and ideas about what you would like to see published.

Visit our website at www.redwheelweiser.com to learn about our upcoming books and free downloads, and be sure to go to *www.redwheelweiser.com/newsletter* to sign up for newsletters and exclusive offers.

You can also contact us at *info@rwwbooks.com*.

Conari Press

an imprint of Red Wheel/Weiser, LLC

65 Parker Street, Suite 7

Newburyport, MA 01950

www.redwheelweiser.com